AMERICAN FOOL

AMERICAN FOOL

THE ROOTS AND IMPROBABLE RISE OF
John Cougar Mellencamp

by MARTIN TORGOFF

Produced by Gelles-Cole Literary Enterprises

ST. MARTIN'S PRESS   NEW YORK

AMERICAN FOOL

Copyright © 1986 by Martin Torgoff. All rights reserved. Printed in the United States of America. No part of this book may be used or reproduced in any manner whatsoever without written permission except in the case of brief quotations embodied in critical articles or reviews. For information, address St. Martin's Press, 175 Fifth Avenue, New York, N.Y. 10010.

Library of Congress Cataloging in Publication Data

Torgoff, Martin.
    American fool.

    1. Mellencamp, John Cougar.   2. Rock musicians—United States—Bibliography.   I. Title.
ML420.M357T7   1986   784.5′4′00924   [B]   85-25108
ISBN 0-312-02319-7 (pbk.)

Design by Stanley S. Drate/Folio Graphics Co. Inc.

FIRST EDITION

10 9 8 7 6 5 4 3 2 1

ACKNOWLEDGMENTS

Many people have given generously of their time, their energy, their moral support, and their talents for this book. Thanks to Ken Aronoff, Jeb Brien, Howard Bloom, Gary Boebinger, Jill Buckler, Martin Cerf, Chris Connelly, A. J. Correale, Bill Cataldo, Mary "Toots" Mellencamp Cowles, Larry Crane, Fay Cummins, Tony DeFries, Len Epand, Tim Elsner, Simon Fields, Don Gehman, Greg Geller, George Green, Bill Hard, France Harper, Jerry Jaffe, Dave Knotts, Kid Leo, Dave Loncao, Michelle Mellencamp, Richard Mellencamp, Ted Mellencamp, Toby Myers, John Prine, Sherry Ring Ginsberg, Mark Ripley, Marolyn Schwartz, Jon Scott, Russel Shaw, Norman Seeff, Tony Tingle, Jody Miller, and Mike Wanchic.

James J. C. "Jamie" Andrews of MainMan Ltd., who passed away during the writing of this book, provided invaluable interviews and photographs. We shall all miss him.

Very special thanks to four lovely women who all bear the same last name, but who weren't born with it: Laura Noblitt Mellencamp, Marilyn Lowe Mellencamp, Priscilla Esterline Mellencamp, and Victoria Granucci Mellencamp.

Another special note of thanks goes to my friend, editor, and agent, Sandi Gelles-Cole, a deft, high-strung, and caring lady who edited my first book six years ago and, for reasons that remain unfathomable, has never ceased to believe in my future.

And goodness!—let me not forget those long-suffering benefactors among my friends and family, who always end up lending me an understanding ear—not to mention money—whenever I undertake the insanity of writing a book: Bess and Irv Torgoff, Matthew and Carol Ash, Merry Aronson, Ed Johnson, Larry Joshua, and Sharon Gabet.

I'm also much obliged to Bob Miller of St. Martin's Press for signing this baby up.

Martin Torgoff
New York City
April 1985

This book is dedicated to:

John Mellencamp, a good egg with a
big heart and more guts than most,
who allowed me to write this book
without ever trying to tell me what
to write;

Larry Joshua, a friend of mine
who is cut from the same cloth;

and Jesse Ash, my nephew—
rock's next generation.

One thing is obvious. The son of a
bitch, considered as a type, has
vitality. He's a dasher, a smasher,
a leaper. There's promise in a son
of a bitch. When you go to buy a
puppy, you know, you're not
supposed to take the sweet one
that licks your hand. You're supposed to take the most rambunc-
tious rascal of the litter, the one
that's roaring around, tearing the
furniture, messing in the middle of
the carpet, giving all the other
pups hell. . . .

—Herman Wouk
Marjorie Morningstar

April 1957

AMERICAN FOOL

PREFACE

It felt good opening up for the Who on their final tour of America. John Cougar had been an opening act for years now, and the role was one he felt particularly in tune with; it required juicing up the crowd, warming them up for the headliner—it was tailor-made for born upstarts and rabblerousers. He was dancing up the stage scaffolding when the beer bottle came humming out of nowhere and—*thunk!*—conked him on the head. As he sank to his knees, eyes rolling in his head, everything went blurry, then black; the band members huddled around him. "Shit, he's out cold." The crowd of fifty thousand souls who had jammed Sun Devil Stadium in Tempe, Arizona, watched in horror as they carried him offstage.

Standing up there, gazing into the glare of the stage lights against the darkness of the vast stadium, he could never have seen it coming. These flying objects come raining down from the balconies of rock palaces, landing at your feet, whizzing by, ricocheting off your body, your guitar—missives of every emotion and impression that people in the audience feel but cannot personally articulate to the performer. There are pins, bottlecaps, candies, and small change (*Here I am*); roses and articles of lingerie from women (*I love you and I wanna fuck your brains out*); and the more menacing missiles like empty Bud bottles, hurled by people whose minds are too dim or trashed out to know better, or with malice aforethought by people who know exactly what they're doing (*I hate you and don't let me get my hands on you*).

Once, in the very beginning, Cougar and his band had been spat upon so mercilessly and with such disgusting velocity by the audience that they'd had to leave the stage. But that was a long time ago, way before he had almost decided to quit this crazy business and to just go off and live with the woman he loved. Now he had the No. 1 song in the country, but the reality of it still hadn't hit him because he'd been on the road forever and people were still giving him shit, writing that it was all a fluke and that he was no good. Sometimes the frustration would bubble up inside him like a poisonous vapor, and he would say things that were ill-advised, rash—there were warrants out for his arrest in three states for profanity onstage (okay, he curses a lot). Not too long ago he'd stormed off a late-night talk show in New York because the woman had turned the interview into an inquisition about his video for a song, treating it like some kind of anthem to sadomasochism, when in fact it was as harmless as a rock & roll version of "The Alley Cat." Millions of people who watched the show were thinking, "What's *his* problem? He's *only* got the best-selling album in the country." Now that the press was finally asking him what his songs really meant, he kept saying, "Nothing . . . they're just some dumb lines I jotted down," downplaying the importance of it all, decrying the incredible pretentiousness of the whole scene; and when several critics started calling him "a true populist poet," he just shrugged his shoulders. But the truth of it was that, deep down, he was trying to decipher the meaning of it all, the way it was all turning around for him after so many years, because he was smart enough to know that what he'd wanted most all along was to break through and soar to the height of his true potential—to a place where his music would be informed and fueled by its most natural feelings and inspirations. . . . People were actually singing the words to his songs at the shows, which flattered him beyond words. Recently, at a show in San Francisco, a biker at the edge of the stage who knew that he loved Harleys had slipped off his black leather jacket—obviously his most prized possession—and had handed it up to him like some totemic offering. Cougar had put on the jacket and worn it during the performance, but then the guy wouldn't take it back. "No, you don't understand—I want you to *have* it. You're the first real rock and roller since Ronnie Van Zandt died," the biker told him. The gift had touched him deeply.

Fuhk, he muttered to himself, as he slowly came around. A doctor was ministering to the throbbing gash in the side of his head as the faces around him came into focus: Vicky, Ted, the guys in the band, the roadies . . .

"You okay?"

Sitting up, he heard the impatient din of the crowd and wanted to know who had thrown the bottle. "Some asshole," he was told by one of the crew.

"Easy," the doctor told him, but he was pissed off—and felt an inexplicable twinge of happiness, sort of like when you get decked in a good football game. He dragged himself to his feet, muzzy-headed and wobbly in the legs, and took a few deep breaths; a rush of energy jolted his body, and his head cleared.

"Hey, lemme borrow that for a few minutes," he said, taking a construction hardhat off one of the stagehands, and putting it on. Before anyone could object, he leaped back onstage and strode defiantly to the microphone, blood streaming down the side of his head, to sing "Hurts So Good." When it was over, the applause was deafening, a thunderous, ever-rising roar that washed over him in wave after wave. Then, of course, he was rushed to the hospital for suturing.

When asked about the incident later on, Cougar quipped, "Now I finally understand what the hell the song means!" What he really meant was that he cared about it all, more deeply than he'd ever admit.

At the time of our first encounter John was lying low after the *American Fool* LP had shocked everyone by becoming the best-selling album of 1982 on the strength of two hit singles, "Hurts So Good" and "Jack and Diane." The first song had miraculously lodged at No. 1 for weeks on end, while the second one climbed to No. 5, making him the first artist to achieve two simultaneous Top Ten tunes since the glory days of the Beatles. But that wasn't why I'd come to Indiana from New York: You learn from experience that the most enjoyable subjects to interview are the ones who evoke in you that sense of deep personal recognition—the intuitive sense that, yes, I *know* this person. We were, after all, the same age—graduates of the high school class of 1970, the year of the first draft lottery for the Vietnam war. Both of us had come of age during that peculiar time warp in American history when the sixties were fading and the seventies had yet to take shape and color; as such, we belonged to one decade or the other, or neither, or both. I came to interview John Mellencamp because, regardless of how different our experience of life had been, I knew we'd have a lot to talk about, and I suspected that he would make me laugh. I was right on both accounts.

To get to where he was then living, you took Route 446 outside of Bloomington, that lazy little Hoosier college town where Peter Yates had filmed *Breaking Away,* and followed the road as it banked its way through verdant rolling hills, past clapboard barns and catfish stands, until you reached a winding curve; it was easy to recognize his place by the enormous satellite dish stationed out front for television reception, and by the telltale collection of vehicles: a pickup truck, a little red Corvette, a gaggle of motorcycles. Here, in a three-story redwood dwelling built into the wooded hillside, lived John "Cougar" Mellencamp—Indiana's favorite rock & roll son. Dressed in a baggy black sweatshirt, with that long shock of brown hair swooping down across gimlet blue eyes and a cobra earring dangling from his left ear, John looked exactly as *People* had described him in a recent profile:

"Like an actor supplied by Central Casting to play the part of a hard-living rocker on a ride to oblivion." (I would soon find out, of course, that the closest John Mellencamp ever came to "hard living" these days was drinking too much Big Red soda.) Small but compact, he had a pugnacity to his demeanor, to his very gait, that suggested James Cagney much more than James Dean, to whom he'd been compared scores of times in the press. Bent forward on his couch, elbows resting on bare knees protruding from a pair of jeans so tattered that they appeared to decompose with the passing minutes, he lit the first of an endless stream of Marlboros and blew a couple of perfectly formed smoke rings so emphatically that the gesture seemed almost violent.

"In songs like 'Jack and Diane,' " I began, "you write nostalgically about growing up in Indiana, but from what I've read about you, your youth didn't seem like such a bargain: You stuttered, you got into a lot of trouble, and you got your ass kicked a lot . . ."

"Hey," John laughed, "you didn't get my *high school* records too, did you?"

"Isn't it true that you were known as a bad egg when you were growing up in Seymour?"

"Well," he exclaimed, *"bad* for Seymour was if you had hair over your ear or if you pissed outdoors! You're dealing with a town that was barbecues in the evenings and church on Sunday. A strict little fucking place . . ."

"Has your family come to grips with what's happened to you?"

John Cougar Mellencamp just stared at me for a moment, a look of peevish bemusement on his face.

"What what's *happened?* Did I *die* or something? Oh, you mean being successful . . ." He grinned wickedly. "Well, I think they think it's just a temporary phase. This year he's big—next year he'll be right back where he started."

Like so many of his adolescent heroes who had conquered the world with electric guitars, John Mellencamp turned his back on the conventional American Dream at a very young age. Instead, he reached for the rock & roll version of that dream, which he clutched and pawed at for ten years, watching as it nearly broke his heart. But for reasons that this book seeks to fathom, he refused to lay down. He set his sights on one step up at a time and dug in his heels and fought the world. Another record, a good song, a song on the charts, a song at the *top* of the charts, a hit album, a Grammy, the critical acclaim that had always eluded him—one by one, he surmounted each obstacle through sheer will, tenacity, the power of his personality, and his ever-developing talent. He succeeded despite the odds, despite the prevailing fashions of the times—despite, even, himself. Now in his early thirties, he has fame, fortune, and creative freedom. The rise of John Mellencamp is a classic American success story, but one rather unique to the experience of his particular generation: By the time he finally made it big, he'd been through so much hell, and had worked so arduously for it, that he had few illusions left about these dreams. In a way, it's really a portrait of every aimless kid who ever stood on a streetcorner and refused to play by the rules, the story of how an anomic misfit from a small town in the Midwest, who knew that he could never make it in the straight world of grades and jobs and drove his parents berserk by playing rock & roll in the garage, grew up to become a poet, a mature artist— an American original.

I

YOUNG BOY DAYS

Wherein Jacky Collects His Thoughts for a Moment, Scratches His Head, and Does His Best James Dean

Everything is slower here
Everybody's got a union card

They get up Sunday, go to church
Come back home, cook out in the backyard

And they call this the Great Midwest
Where the cornfields row and flow

They're all five years ahead of their time
Or twenty-five behind, I just don't know

—"The Great Midwest"

To walk the peaceful, treelined streets of Seymour on a drowsy summer day is to realize that Andy Hardy lived in a place like this; to stand at the corner of Chestnut and Second streets, the nexus of its civilization, and simply watch the people go by, is to recognize the characters from the short stories of Sherwood Anderson, the poems of Edgar Lee Masters, the illustrations of Norman Rockwell.

Touted as the "crossroads of southern Indiana" by the local chamber of commerce, the town grew up at the junction of the B&O and Pennsylvania railways, ninety miles west of Cincinnati, between Indianapolis and Louisville, Kentucky. Seymour's historical claim to fame is the fabled Reno Brothers—Frank, Bill, and Simeon—who, in 1866, pulled off America's first train robbery. The gently rolling landscape of this part of the state is dotted with one-horse, hole-in-the-wall towns, with names like Deputy, Surprise, Hope, and Acme, which make Seymour, with its thirty churches, fifteen bars,

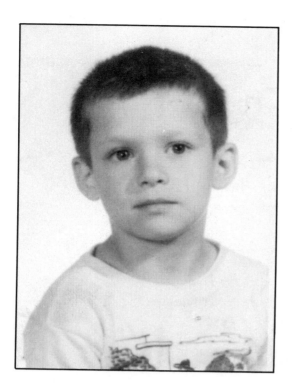

John Mellencamp, 1957.

four parks, and a hospital, look like a sprawling metropolis. The land that surrounds the town is flat and lush, filled with feed barns and moldering shacks and hardworking farmers whose net worth is always measured in acres planted.

Besides agriculture, people's minds around here tend toward patriotism (*Join the Marines, Visit Exotic Lands, Kill Exotic People* reads the T-shirt of one crew-cut youth hanging out in front of Hook's Drug), conservative politics, religion ("Christianity" is a popular name for baby girls in born-again families these days), basketball (Hoosier Larry Bird, that "hick from French Lick" who plays for the Boston Celtics, is revered as a Great American), football (ah, those hapless Indianapolis Colts), drinking, cars, motorcycles, sex, and fisticuffs. Yes, this is southern Indiana, folks, where the accent is a cross between a nasal twang and a southern drawl and speech is peppered with a lot of "fuhks" and "goddamns"—the land of James Dean, the Ku Klux Klan, pickup trucks, Tastee Freez, the Indy 500, church socials, boilermakers, Bobby Knight, John Deere, trailer parks, pigs, corn, Wonder Bread sandwiches with the crusts cut off, bugs the size of your thumb, winding rivers, covered bridges, polyester leisure suits, faded denim overalls, smokestacks, unemployment, country music, marriage at eighteen . . . blue eyes and cornsilk blond hair and milk-fed pale skin . . . Jack and Diane and little pink houses for you and me.

Although Seymour may have looked like the quintessence of Main Street, USA, it had its slimy underside. During the 1970s, a corrupt mayor had turned the town into a massive chemical dumpsite, making Seymour one of the most toxic spots in the nation. For a while, the town also had the distinction of having the highest per-capita murder rate in the United States. Although this climate may have contributed to the child's sense of hyperrebelliousness, to his lifelong contempt for authority figures of every kind, John himself is more likely to trace this aspect of his character back to his family. He calls it "that Bad Mellencamp Family Attitude." "My father has it," he says, "and Grandpa had it too; and so, probably, did my great-grandfather . . ."

The original John Mellencamp came to the United States in the late 1800s, fleeing the Kaiser's system of military conscription and looking for a good tract of land. According to Richard Mellencamp, the present John's father, "my people were German peasant farmers from outside of Hamburg."

With ten children, John Mellencamp was poor but stubbornly proud—a trait that would become central to the Mellencamp family identity. "My grandfather had a gall bladder attack in 1924 and died because the family couldn't pay the medical bill," recounts Richard Mellencamp. "They didn't have the money for the operation, they couldn't borrow it, so they elected to let him die."

After the death, the family fell on hard times. Harry Perry Mellencamp, or "Speck" as he came to be known, had to quit school before he reached the third grade and go to work so that his family could eat. Speck Mellencamp was determined not to make his living off the land, however, but with his hands, as a carpenter. Handsome, wiry, and fierce, he married a sweet, blue-eyed girl named Laura Noblitt and settled down to raise a family, only to see his house lost in 1930, at the nadir of the Great Depression. But like his father before him, Speck Mellencamp's sense of pride and honor were paramount. "He would never take charity or welfare," Grandma Laura says. "He'd say, 'Forget it! We're not that poor that we have to live off the government.' He wouldn't let us take secondhand clothes, either. Sometimes he was too proud for his own good." "When Grandpa went to vote once, the woman at the polling booth made fun of his name," John relates. "He never voted for the rest of his life because of that incident."

By all accounts, Speck Mellencamp also had an explosive temper. He demanded respect, and if he did not get it, his fists spoke like a double-barrel

Young Richard Mellencamp.

shotgun. "If you said something to Grandpa that he didn't like," John says, "he wouldn't discuss it with you—he'd just beat your ass." Yet, at the same time, Speck was a tenderhearted man, devoted to his wife and six children. These qualities made the Mellencamps something of an enigma to the townspeople of Seymour. Because of their arrogant pride, their clannishness, their it's-us-against-the-world mentality, they began to develop a reputation as outsiders. Toots, the oldest, was pretty but tough—a wild country girl, a tomboy. The two oldest boys, Joe and Richard, were roughnecks—Joe, a strapping football star at Indiana University, had a reputation as the toughest boxer in southern Indiana. Richard, who was smaller, was no less combative and had to try harder, it seemed, to live up to the Mellencamp reputation. Competition became his particular ethos, his lifelong avocation. In his youth its most striking dividend came in the form of the girl he would marry, Marilyn Lowe.

If John Mellencamp gets his toughness, his honesty, his pride, his sensitivity, and his antisocial behavior from his father's side of the family, he gets a whole different set of traits from his mother's. Since colonial times, the Lowes had lived in Jackson and Scott counties, getting their fingers into all kinds of pies. Even today, if you mention the name of John's grandfather, Joe Lowe—in Austin, Indiana, heads turn. Bootlegger, scammer, moneyman, beer-bellied bon vivant, Joe Lowe owned and operated a restaurant in Austin that also functioned as a poolroom, a gambling parlor, and a speakeasy, complete with slot machines. He was also a famous bullshitter, a master of the fine art of rodomontade—the telling of tall tales with a perfectly straight face.

One story still told about his establishment dates from World War II, when the government brought in German POWs to man the town's factory. Naturally, the GIs who had to guard them became regulars at Joe's, and at the end of the war, a bunch of them approached him before shipping out. "We just wanted to tell you, Joe, that we've been putting all the salt in the sugar dispensers, and the sugar in the salt shakers," they told him, "but because we like you, we won't do it this last week." "Hell," Joe said disconsolately, "I guess that means I'll have to stop spitting in your coffee cups."

Because the disparity between rich and poor was so pronounced in Austin, and because her father belonged to its tiny entrepreneurial middle class—he was one of a handful of people to own a car—Marilyn Lowe grew up with a deeply ingrained desire to be among the haves instead of the have-nots. "When one person runs the town and everyone else is down under, you never lose that feeling," she says today. She was determined to dress well, to have nice things—in short, to have status. When she went away to the School of Elementary Education at Indiana University, she confides, "I never used to want my friends to know I was from that little hick town."

One thing that set Marilyn apart from the crowd was her looks—she was a knockout, and she knew it. Small but curvaceous, with large brown eyes and dark, lustrous hair, she was the queen of the Scott County Fair and the runnerup for Miss Indiana in 1946. She also had a good singing voice, though she had no intention of using it for a career. "Somebody was always after me to do it. I'd get paid $50 to come to the Lions' Club in Indianapolis. That was a lot of money in those days, but there was a negative attitude about singing in clubs. Too many dirty old men . . ."

There was also talk about how Marilyn had "gone to Hollywood" to make it in the movies; in truth, she'd gone out there to visit her Uncle Bill. "My father spread it around that I was going to be a star," she laughs. "It was one of his lies." Nonetheless, the rumor added to her allure, to the notion that Marilyn Lowe was somehow different from other people in Austin. "I put on airs," she says. "I guess I was stuck up. And you know what? I still am."

Before long, Marilyn Lowe married her high school sweetheart and had a baby boy, Joe, a marriage that lasted only six months.

The first time Marilyn Lowe saw Richard Mellencamp, he was about to be arrested. "It was in Scottsburg," she recalls, "and I saw this police light flashing. The two Mellencamp boys had gotten into a fight and beat up on a bunch of guys. Joe was being hauled off to jail, but Richard had somehow talked his way out of it. I didn't think too much of the Mellencamps . . ."

Richard had noticed her, however, and was smitten. "I thought he was just

some hillbilly," she says. "But when I got to know him, I began to see how nice he was. He was very bright, very ambitious." They started dating and were married in six months. Richard was twenty at the time, Marilyn several years older, with a toddler. At first the Mellencamp clan was wary of the marriage, but it was a perfect match. Despite his wild streak, more than anything Richard Mellencamp wanted the good life for his family, and to make Mellencamp a name to be reckoned with in the community. And if he should ever waver or falter, he now also had Marilyn Mellencamp—no shrinking violet—spurring him on.

Meninges cele is a potentially fatal condition that occurs before birth, when one of the vertebrae of a fetus fails to fuse. Fluid becomes sealed on the outside of the spine, which can cause the infant to be crippled, without the use of a limb, or worse. In the case of John Mellencamp, born on October 7, 1951, the deformity took the form of a growth that stretched from his back to the base of his skull, completely covering his neck—John would describe it as "the size of a man's fist" in a 1983 article in *People*. At first the prognosis for Richard and Marilyn's first child was gloomy. "When I first saw him, I almost died," Marilyn confides. "Here was this beautiful baby with this horrible deformity. They didn't know what the neurological implications were going to be."

To make things worse, Richard had been drafted into the Air Force and was stationed in Columbus, Georgia. After consultation with specialists, Marilyn took John to the Indiana University Medical Center for an operation to remove the growth and to fuse his spine. He was six weeks old and would remain in the hospital for another six weeks. The operation would prove a complete success, with no lasting physical effects, though Marilyn recognizes that the experience must have traumatized her son. "When he'd get wild as an infant and then as a child, I'd wonder how much it had to do with those six weeks when he was denied his mother in the hospital, from hearing my voice and feeling my touch. And if there was ever a child who demanded attention, it was John—and if he couldn't get it from me when my other children came along, he was going to get it elsewhere."

With Richard's discharge in 1953 and the birth of Ted Mellencamp, the family bought a house in Seymour, at 714 West Fifth Street, and Richard settled down to begin his long, inexorable climb to success. He began by

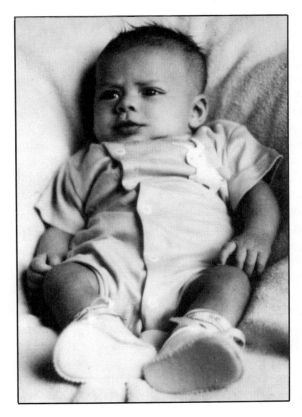

John, displaying that Bad Mellencamp Family Attitude.

Age four, as mascot of the Seymour High football team.

attending electrical school for four years in Indianapolis, then landed a job with Robbins Electric. Working ten-to-fourteen-hour days, six to seven days a week, he rose to supervisor, eventually went into the office as an estimator, and finally made his way into the executive boardroom as a vice president. "It meant that I wasn't home that much," he says. "Marilyn really raised the children."

With three boys and the subsequent births of two girls, Janet and Laura, Marilyn Mellencamp had her hands full. Her task was compounded by the personalities of John and Ted—"problem" kids in the classic sense. John had developed a stuttering that, combined with the aftereffects of the operation and his natural Bad Mellencamp Family Attitude, made him one ornery, obstreperous little tyke. "Let's put it this way," John laughs. "When I was a kid, *I* wouldn't have liked me!"

Snapshots galore of the Mellencamp kids exist from this period, when the family lived on Fifth Street; and no matter how old John is in these photos, he either looks like an angel or a suspect in a police line-up. There was always the unmistakable twinkle of mischief in his eyes. Indeed, there was one of him in every school—the five-year-old desperado, the kid who used the bad word (the dreaded "f" curse!) and, upon noticing the pandemonium it provoked in the classroom and the swift and terrible retribution from the teacher, only did it again and again. You know, the sort of kid who made his mother cry. "In all his class pictures he'd always be standing next to the teacher," Marilyn

At the front of the line, already sporting a motorcyclist's cap, John leads his first grade class on a trip to Vernon, Indiana.

recalls, "and I could never figure out if it was because he was the teacher's pet or because he was such a little maniac. But he *was* cute . . ."

At the age of four, he became the mascot of Dave Shaw's Seymour High football team. Shaw later recalled this "good-looking little fella showing up for football practice" to an interviewer from *Indianapolis Magazine*. "Every time we were there practicing, he'd be there. As time went on, he began running wind sprints with us. One day he came with a football jersey, a pair of practice pants, and headgear like the rest of the guys. So we kind of adopted him."

Even at that young age, observes Marilyn, "John had this attitude when he walked down the street that said, *Watch out! I am somebody so you'd better get out of my way!* It was this strut, this kind of swagger that all the Mellencamp men have—elbows out, arms swinging, chest all puffed out, fists clenched. I'd go to give him a kiss, and he'd scrunch up his sweet little face like I was going to *poison* him—it wasn't 'cool.' Boy, he could be a mean little cuss. He'd take a stick and whack the patrol girls on the legs real hard. Then when the principal, Mr. Estal, complained about it, John just hit him with the stick, too!"

"Hell, he was about five or six, not even in school yet," remembers Gary Boebinger, who lived not far from the Mellencamps, "and me and my friends were about ten or eleven, and he'd come out of his house and throw rocks at us! It was like an obstacle course getting to school because of this little kid out

John and brother Ted (right).

on the lawn. Most little kids would be afraid of the 'big' guys, but his attitude was, 'Attack!' ''

"If I'm a good songwriter, it's because I'm a good liar," states John. "I did so much lying as a kid I got good at it. I was one of those kids who would do something unspeakable and then, when I was about to get caught, I could put this expression on my face and say, 'Wait a minute! This ain't what you think . . .' and somehow get out of it."

Methods of evasion didn't always work, however. "There was this barn up on this hill," says Ted Mellencamp. "We were about nine or ten, and the best thing we could think of doing was to take walnuts and throw them and break out the windows. Had a great time; they'd replace the windows and we'd just go break 'em out again. One night we were all sitting around the table eating dinner and there was a knock at the door. It was the city police. There we were, being handcuffed and put in the back of the squad car, being taken downtown . . ." Today, the incident brings a smile to the face of Richard Mellencamp. "We went along with that just to scare the hell out of them—they thought they were going off to jail. We wanted to teach them a lesson."

The lesson, however, would not easily take hold.

"When Dad started making his money," Ted Mellencamp remembers, "he went to the Cadillac dealer in Seymour to buy his first Caddy, and the guy said to him, 'You can't afford one of these cars.' I guess their attitude was, hell, the Mellencamps were just a bunch of poor people from out around Woodstock, the poor part of town—they shouldn't be driving Caddys! So he went to

Indianapolis to get one; then, he bought another. The bank wouldn't let him bid on a house that was for sale when we wanted to move, so he went and bought the biggest house in town. He was going to just sit out there and say fuck you to everybody."

The house was just outside of town, a stately, white, two-story affair complete with a circular driveway, surrounded by several wooded acres of land. It was the Mellencamp's Tara, their Graceland mansion. "I wanted a big house where we could all have a lot of space," Marilyn explains. "It was a big step up for us." The place may have looked like an estate, but thirty years of neglect had left it in a state of dilapidation. "Mom and Dad were going to refurbish the place with cheap child coolie labor," offers Ted. "We had to sand the walls and cut all the wood and everything. We worked all the time, every night."

Any friend of the Mellencamp kids who ventured out there did so at his own risk. "John would call me on a Saturday," says Mark Ripley, one of his closest friends, "and you'd get out there to find some godawful job to do. 'Well, don't just stand there, Ripley, get busy!' One time we were clearing away lumber, and John threw a log without looking and hit Ted right in the side of the head. Ted went nuts and grabbed an ax and chased him around the yard—I swear, he was going to *ax* him . . ."

They were wild, these Mellencamps—boisterous, unruly, rivalrous, and very physical. "That was our way of showing love," John reflects. "We were never really taught to express affection other ways." It was also part of the competitive ethic that Richard tried to instill in his children as a means of preparing them for the struggles of life. He pitted the three boys against each other in an endless series of athletic competitions: footraces, pushup and chinning contests, boxing matches. "Dad groomed us to be macho," John says. "He was a jock in high school, and he pushed us real hard. 'You're a *Mellencamp,* you try harder.' "

In the summertime, the boys were expected to work with Uncle Joe's construction outfit, pouring concrete. Uncle Joe was a firm believer in "toughening the boys up for football" and paid special attention to John, because he was small. He'd load up a wheelbarrow with heavy rocks. "Come on, John, run with it, *move!*" At lunchtime, he'd make John eat his sandwich out in the hot sun—"It'll give you *stamina!*" And then there was the famous balancing drill: While Uncle Joe went hurtling down some bumpy country road, John would walk out onto the heavy wooden planks that dragged behind the truck used for pouring the concrete into curbs and such, and ride them like a surfboard. "The trick was not to fall off the planks and bust your skull open on the pavement!" explains John.

When disputes arose among the boys, Richard's philosophy was to take them out into the backyard, put the boxing gloves on them, and simply let them beat each other's brains out. "They'd establish their natural pecking order that way," Richard says in retrospect. "I don't know if it was the right way, but I don't think it hurt them either . . . And it certainly *was* entertaining!"

Within the rigorously disciplined household, these riotous brawls represented quite a departure from the normal regime. Marilyn was a tough top sergeant when it came to running the house, and the chores that John Mellencamp spent the greater part of his youth trying to avoid were systematically distributed to the kids—even the ironing of clothes. "Every night we had to be there for dinner," John says. "On Sundays it was mandatory to go to the Nazarene Church, which was Grandma's strict old church. It was either that or you got beat. Mom and I sort of got into a bad habit with each other. She'd say, 'I'm your mother, and you *have* to listen to me'; and my attitude was, 'What gives you the right to tell me what to do?' "

"I fight authority/Authority always wins," is the way John would express his lifelong rebellion in a song so many years later. He could get around his mother by sniping, carping, whining, manipulating—but when Richard came home, well, the jig was up, for the simple reason that "he could whip my ass." And whip it he did. "It wasn't just a shaking," Ted reveals. "We'd get hit in the face. John was a faster runner than me—the old man couldn't catch him quite so easily. But in the end, he always did."

The two older Mellencamp boys, Joe and John, were turning out to be a study in contrast. John hated school and made lousy grades, Joe loved it and excelled scholastically; John hated going to church, Joe sang in the choir; John kicked and screamed every time he had to mow the lawn, whereas Joe performed the task with nary a whimper of complaint. It was easy to see why Joe, adopted by Richard Mellencamp at the age of seven, occupied a special place in Mom's heart. "Joe was the type of kid who always had the lead in the school play," Mark Ripley notes. "John, on the other hand, who had to compete with Joe, played the small part of the military man in our freshman class production of *Li'l Abner*. He was supposed to come out and say, 'Clear Dogpatch!' Of course, when his moment came, he was jacking around backstage, trying to talk to some girl. 'Man, you're on!' He ran out there in front of everybody and went completely blank. One line and he couldn't remember it . . ."

But Ted Mellencamp was the real problem child of the family—completely ungovernable, a bona-fide vandal. "Ted was in trouble *all* the time," says Richard Mellencamp. "The difference between John and Ted was that John was in trouble with *us* a lot, but Ted was really *in trouble*. Marilyn had to spend a lot of time with him." True, Ted did crazy things that worried his folks, like the time he vandalized an entire lot of combines at the John Deere plant just for something to do. The upshot was that John Mellencamp had to turn elsewhere for the attention he wanted, usually to Grandma and Grandpa. Indeed, from the moment of his birth, Laura Mellencamp had paid special attention to John, recognizing the vulnerable, creative side of her grandson at a very young age. "I babied him a lot," she admits. "He was real sensitive. He really thought about things a lot and he'd meditate about them and always ask us what we thought. That's the kind of kid he was."

As the intimacy and trust increased between John and Grandma, she began to play the role of his diplomat within the family, which drove Marilyn Mellencamp up the wall. "She spoiled him rotten," Marilyn insists. "He was her favorite, and some of the others resented it because she'd spend 100 percent of her time with him. And no matter what I was doing to try and give him some constructive advice about growing up, she'd tell him, 'Now don't worry, John, your mom just doesn't *understand* yet. One day, she will.' Of course, John ate it up."

(left to right) Ted, John, little Laura, Janet, and the indomitable Marilyn Mellencamp.

Without a doubt, the most important person in John's life was the patriarch of the family, Speck Mellencamp. John admired Speck's simple dignity, his self-reliance, his belligerent pride. The brightest moments of his childhood came when he would get to go off with Grandpa on some job, and John would listen raptly while the lean, work-hardened old man would teach him carpentry and extol the virtues of good, old-fashioned quality craftsmanship. "Grandpa was my role model," John recognizes, "the most influential person in the family. He never needed to prove anything to anybody."

The milestones of growing up in Indiana came at three ages: sixteen, when you could get a license to drive; eighteen, when you no longer had to abide by the statewide curfew and be off the streets by eleven o'clock; and twenty-one, when you could just about do anything you damn well pleased. John Mellencamp's watershed moments—actually the crucial events of his adolescence—were more personal, like the day football coach Dick Mace saw a pack of Marlboros sticking brazenly out of his back pocket and screamed, "You're off the team, Mellencamp!" Up until that time, John had been a pretty serious athlete. He ran track and even held the school record for the hundred-yard dash for a while—he liked to run the cinder track barefoot, to show off in front of the girls. But football was his main sport, despite his size. "That snotty-nosed little kid could *run*," Coach Thomas recalled in a Cinemax documentary in 1984. Coach Knight, speaking for the news cameras of WISH-TV in 1983, remembered him as being "all boy. But he did a lot of stupid things and was always on the verge of being in trouble. He clowned around and liked to present the image of being a rebel, a nonconformist, and a . . . *hood*."

That was the key word: *hood*. A vague attitude, a look, a slouch that usually meant one thing: *fuck you, baby*. Throughout John's adolescence, the look of it was defined more and more in movies on television and on the screens of the old Seymour theaters, like the Majestic. It was Brando's leather jacket swagger in *The Wild One* and James Dean's sullen teen angst in *Rebel Without a Cause*. Other influences began to trickle in: Lenny Bruce's profanity, the sneering stance of rock & roll bad boys like Gene Vincent. "I didn't know what these people *did* hardly, but I liked the way they looked," John tries to explain. "I had no respect for anything. When I saw Paul Newman as Hud, I dug the character he played—I thought he was cool—I had no idea he was this really abusive jerk! There was this older guy in Seymour who used to clip school and hang out drunk on the streetcorners; I decided I wanted to be like *him* . . . I remember being told you can't wear metal taps on your shoes in school because they clicked when you walked down the hall. My attitude was, 'Well, I don't care, I *like* the way they click. Put 'em on there!' "

In small towns like Seymour, it was easy to spot other likeminded kids, because they always stood out like sore thumbs—it was part of the fun. "There was a kid I went to the Nazarene church with," John says. "You weren't allowed to dance or wear jewelry or anything in our church. We used to go to Sunday school and sneak out. Sunday school lasted 45 minutes and then you'd have to go to church for an hour. Well, we would always sneak out of the church section and smoke cigarettes and go to the post office and look at the wanted pictures. This kid went back to the street in front of the church and went nuts, and started calling God an asshole in front of the church and the whole congregation. He shouted at the sky, 'If you're so fucking strong, come on down here and strike me dead, godammit!' Embarrassed his parents to death, right?"

Then, when sitting in the Vondee during his sophomore year in high school, it all came together in one glorious epiphany—the sublime personification of everything he was feeling. The film was *Cool Hand Luke,* one of the most devastating portraits of an individualist (Luke) battling the social system (the chain gang); the scene came when the prison bosses decided that they were finally going to break Luke's spirit through the mindless brutality of physical punishment, making him dig holes and fill them again until he surrendered his free will. The film provided John with a means of declaring war on the system and turning his own life into an act of guerrilla warfare, often treading a thin line between hilarity and outright nightmare, all of it wildly romanticized in his imagination.

"I realized at that point that my destiny was to be a fuck-up. Me and my friends saw that movie a hundred times. We thought we *were* Luke in the movie. We used to go out absolutely defiant. All of us seemed to have one thing in common, some sort of crazy drive. Everything was always in excess. You can't just drink five beers, you've got to drink fifteen. Can't just smoke a little pot, got to smoke a whole bunch. Can't do LSD once . . . got to take it twenty times. Can't have one girl, have to have one a week. To someone who considers himself an intellectual, all this would seem stupid. They'd think the mentality was real low, but it's a real mentality, the real world. In that small town, it was all about having some kind of identity in a place where everyone else was the same, did things the same way."

These rampageous teenage years were the most fanciful of John's life—a time of madcap fun and adventure that would later provide him with fertile material. "You never really understand the saying, Youth is wasted on the young, until you look back," he says. "It all seemed like this great big Cinemascope adventure we were living in . . ." You could see them standing in front of the Seymour National Bank, at the corner of Second and Chestnut,

Archetypal teenaged influences: Brando as "Johnny" in *The Wild One;* Dean as Jim Stark in *Rebel Without A Cause;* and Paul Newman as *Cool Hand Luke.*

sometimes twenty of them standing around smoking cigarettes, easy targets for the cops to chase once the town's eleven o'clock curfew went into effect. After school they'd all be in Marilyn's Coffee Shop, smoking cigarettes and eating grilled cheese sandwiches with french fries and drinking Big Red (they called it "Red Eye"), a fulsome soda with the sweet, heavy taste of bubble gum that is brewed in Texas. Their patented uniform included Bass Weejun loafers, severely ironed chino pants with little cuffs, and belts with shotgun shells—the typical collegiate outfit of the mid-1960s—except for the obvious fact of their ducktails and Boston blacks and other deranged hairstyles. In fact, John had already peroxided his hair by junior high school—"My parents had a fit"—and would one day write a song about this called "The Great Midwest": "We're either five years ahead of our time or twenty-five behind," the song goes. "I just don't know."

"We were the ones getting kicked out of basketball games for fighting," reflects John. "We were the ones getting laid. We were the ones smoking marijuana before it was fashionable." Of course, in a town as small as Seymour everybody knows everything about everybody else's business and word about John and the boys spread quickly. "Don't be hangin' around with that Mellencamp kid," parents would admonish their children before they went out at night. "He'll get you arrested."

The one thing that the boys all had in common was that their parents were thoroughly ashamed of them. To make the Seymour High honor roll, you needed sixteen points; the boys, however, had their own honor roll: You needed only one point to be included among its venerable ranks. "Knotts once had five Fs and a D," John remembers. "We almost made it a point of getting the worst possible grades because I guess that seemed like the most dangerous thing we could possibly do! What could be worse than throwing away your future?" Nevertheless, they also made a point of all meeting after school on the days report cards were distributed to doctor the grades, changing their Ds to Bs, but their parents usually found out and grounded them. The boys had their means of revenge. "We used to go down to the Elks Club while our parents were inside and roll their cars into each other for fun. Put 'em in neutral and push 'em down the hill—Bam!"

The group of John's feckless friends changed over the years, but the nucleus—those few guys who remain his best friends to this day—stayed pretty much the same. There was Mark Ripley, the local doctor's son, an ungainly, good-natured soul with a rollicking sense of humor, born only a day apart from John (their mothers shared the same hospital room). He devoted his entire adolescence to chasing girls, who were usually terrified at the sight of him; he was known throughout Seymour as the "backseat mauler." "Hey, I saved John's life in high school," Ripley modestly relates. "We were out at the gravel pit swimming out to this little island, and he couldn't swim worth a shit—still can't—and the sonofabitch grabbed me around the neck, and I thought it was double-drowning time. He was panicking and climbed on my shoulders! I got him to the island somehow and just looked at him. 'Well, how you gonna get back now, Johnny?' "

J. D. Nicholson was the all-American boy to whom everything came easy—Robert Redford gone bad. "Jay was real good-looking," John says. "We ran around together a lot because we both wanted the prettiest girls in the town—the cheerleaders and the homecoming queens."

Dave Knotts, another doctor's son, was the one with the car. "The first time I hung out with those guys, they asked me if I wanted to go to a basketball game," Knotts recollects. "Jay went in and swiped a pint of whiskey out of a drugstore and off we went. John was a sophomore—a bit of a braggart and a showoff, but a really nice guy. Always had his mouth going in high volume. One morning we played hookey and stole a case of beer and went and drank it over at J. D.'s house. Then we went back to school. We were all sneaking around the halls, drunk, and John, of course, was going right up to people, breathing in their faces, couldn't wait for somebody to say, 'Oh, you've been *drinking*!' "

The illegal procurement of booze became easy when Pat Mackey, another member of the group, stole a wallet with an ID that fit him perfectly. The bunch of them would pile into a car and head over to Brownstown, where Mack would brazenly enter the Candlelight Tavern, flash the ID saying he was twenty-eight—he was really sixteen—and buy the beer. "I remember going down these Indiana country roads at a hundred miles an hour, with the headlights off and beer spilling all over the place, and Jay holding his hands over his eyes while I was driving," John reminisces. "We cruised to the Four Tops' "Standing in the Shadows of Love," James Brown's "Papa's Got a Brand New Bag," and the Doors' "Hello, I Love You."

After the basketball game, everyone would repair to the basement of a local church for the Last Exit Dance. Then, as curfew time approached, the evening would take on a more frantic quality. It was time to cruise the town, take "the Lap": Drive down Chestnut, past the stores, take a left, proceed down the road in back of the stores, then do it again; get out and lean on a parking meter and watch the cavalcade pass by; run out into the road and howl like banshees into the night and just keep hanging out and hoping for that one girl to come along until the cops appeared and stuck their faces out of the patrol car and said, "Get along, you kids—it's gettin' on curfew." "See, if you're out past curfew, you were illegal anyway," John rationalizes, "so if you did it, you might as well *really* break the law! Yeah, it was always "one more lap . . .""

"There was dancing down at the Armory every weekend," he continues, "and we always went down there to try and pick up girls or fight. I mean, you *had* to fight—your dignity depended on it. In one of my first songs, I wrote, 'If you can't find a lady then start a fight.' It wasn't just me; there were hundreds of us. Sometimes we fought five times a week."

The problem with John Mellencamp and fighting was that he had a loud mouth of legendary proportions ("In high school I never ever knew John had a face because his mouth was always open," recalls one local girl)—and, consequently, due to his rather diminutive size, he was always getting himself into "deep shit." "John used to beat up on all the kids when he started grade school," Richard Mellencamp tells me. "He was bigger than most of the kids. Then one year, all of the other kids grew and John didn't; only his *mouth* never stop growing."

The fateful year came at the age of thirteen, when John reached his optimum size at five-foot-seven, 135 pounds. "I wasn't a tough kid," John says. "I just *thought* I was." At least he never allowed the humiliation of losing a fight to be compounded by the shame of backing down from one. His friends recall the time that John had managed to insult one of the school bullies and then spent the next month or so studiously avoiding the inevitable fight by hiding—underneath stairwells, in alleyways—wherever possible. Finally, the derision of his friends became too degrading for him to handle and a meeting was set up in the school parking lot. (Our boy apparently figured a broken nose was preferable to a reputation as a "chickenshit.") The event was attended by a group of students, all of them standing around like Romans waiting for the Christians to be thrown to the lions. John strolled up as jauntily as possible to his waiting opponent and said, "Okay. Let's get it."

"Mellencamp," his foe taunted. "I'm gonna *kill* you."

The threat must have seemed awfully plausible at that moment, because John had the good sense to say, "There's just one rule. Whoever says I quit first, that's *it*. Okay?"

The first punch of the fight was a colossal right that spoke plainly to John's eye, telling him that the battle was most definitely over. "That's *it*," he cried, almost happily, putting his hands up in submission.

"Mellencamp, I can hit my mother harder than that!"

"Here was the guy with the nice sweaters and the Weejuns," Tim Elsner

Outside his parents house on North Ewing Street, Seymour, age sixteen.

says of John, "talking big, and the other kids—the legitimately tough kids from the wrong side of the tracks—would see him and say, 'Who does this little asshole think he *is*?' " "Oh, yes, he'd piss a lot of people off," Knotts concurs. "But he was pretty fleet of foot, too—he'd do some runnin'! Also, he had J. D. Nicholson backing him, who was handy with his fists. Most people knew that if you were gonna fight John, you'd have to fight Jay."

Sometimes Jay wasn't around, and John had no choice but to stand and fight. He was eighteen years old when he squared off against a galoot named Murray and had the last fistfight of his life. "It was humiliating," recalls John. "The guy got so tired of beating *me* up that he started beating up the car I was driving! He ripped off the radio antenna and smashed in the windshield, the side windows—there was nothing I could do. I think back about it sometimes and laugh, but other times I get sick thinking about it. Thinking, God, can you actually believe I *did* that?"

Certainly, rock & roll seemed like a safer pastime for John Mellencamp, who learned at a very young age that the importance of a good song was how it made you feel and how it related to your life. "My old man did the worst thing he could have done when he gave me a radio back in high school. That was the end of all studying for me."

After supper, when he was supposed to be studying—he was flunking all his courses—John would be upstairs tuning in the big radio stations from Detroit and Chicago. The music that poured forth and filled his fervid imagination was invariably black. "I didn't even know white people made records at first," he says. "If they did, I didn't want to know about it. It was all Sam and Dave, the Temptations, Otis Redding, the Four Tops, and James Brown—that's what I loved. Those were the first records I bought at Sears Roebuck, which is where you shopped for records in Seymour, Indiana."

John became one of a handful of kids in town who became seriously interested in music. At the age of thirteen, he had decided to learn how to play guitar after seeing a local band play at a dance. The leader of the band was a kid named Hubie Ashcraft, who called his band Tikis and played Ventures-style electric guitars, performing songs like the theme from *Peter Gunn*. It was the first time John saw an actual rock band playing live, and he thought it was the greatest thing he'd ever seen in his life. "These were *high school* guys," he marvels, "with bad complexions, girlfriends, and everything else you've always wanted, right? I mean, these guys were *cool.*"

By the age of fourteen, he formed his first band, Crepe Soul, with Fred Booker. Booker, from one of Seymour's twenty-eight black families, was a tall, skinny fellow several years older than John who could dance like a whirlwind. "I'd do my Wayne Cochrane imitation and he would be James Brown," John laughs. "He had the dances down, the cape, everything. Can you *imagine* singing "This Is a Man's World" at fourteen?" "We wore the jackets with the Nehru collars and tight pants with English riding boots," Fred Booker recollected for the 1984 Cinemax documentary, laughing at their audacity. "We thought we were really something."

Crepe Soul played out at Uncle Joe Mellencamp's roller rink a few times and once got a job at brother Joe's frat house up in Bloomington for $30 a weekend. Otherwise, the opportunities were slim. Finally they landed a gig at the raceway bar in Salem, but it didn't last long. "One night a fight broke out and some black guy slashed a white guy with a knife," recalls John, "and we just got the hell out of there fast!"

By then, the world of pop music was ruled by the Beatles and the Rolling Stones, and the particular group you preferred became your badge of identity. "I loved the Stones and disliked the Beatles. I never cared for the guys who looked good. I liked Eric Burdon, who had pimples on his face and a big double chin. Girls would look at him and go, 'Yuk! Eric Burdon!' I loved Mitch Ryder for the same reason. There was always something about these guys that you couldn't quite trust—they were disreputable figures of influence with which we could identify."

By the end of high school, playing in a band had become "much too serious" for John. He hated going to rehearsals and thought that guys who spent all their time in their rooms practicing were suckers, even if he did continue to play at home. "He'd sit in the dining room with his guitar and play for people," Marilyn Mellencamp relates, "and everyone would say, "Hey, he's good!' After high school, somebody heard him sing and offered him a job singing in the dining room of the Ramada Inn in Columbus. It was an expensive place, and the guy was going to pay him $25 a night. John put on a suit and went over and everything went great. The next night he came down in blue jeans and a T-shirt. I said, 'What on *earth* are you doing?' 'Mom,' he says, 'it's bad enough I have to *sing* for those people. I'm not going back out there in some damn monkey suit!' That was the end of that job."

Marilyn could scarcely have understood that her son had long since come under the influence of Bob Dylan; once he had even tried playing "The Times They Are A-Changin' " to try to enlighten her, but the effort proved futile. By that time, John had become like a sponge, soaking up whatever he could of the images and messages in the music he loved. For someone who did not grow up during the 1960s, it's difficult to comprehend the sheer variety of the music that comprised the soundtrack of so many lives, difficult to appreciate the incredible fertility and power of meaning and influence. Think of it!—the earth-shattering impact of Dylan's *Highway 61 Revisited,* Jimi Hendrix's *Are You Experienced?,* Cream's *Disraeli Gears*—moments of sublime teen transcendence that John Mellencamp, like so many others, would never quite recover from. Not many kids in Seymour cared quite so passionately about listening to music as John—the actual playing of it was beside the point, just another way of trying to be cool, different.

"I'd sit outside strumming my guitar and wait for the girls to come by," he says, "and they'd look at me and say, 'Oh, *you* play guitar?' That was the only thing that mattered—the girls."

"He thought he was Bob Bitchen in high school," Mark Ripley insists. "He thought he could pick up any chick in town!" Indeed, John devoted the better part of his adolescence not to school, music, or fighting but to the singleminded pursuit of sex; and, by all accounts, he did so with all the subtlety of a kamikaze pilot heading for an undefended aircraft carrier. "Well, sex is the most important thing in a kid's life," John pronounces with absolute finality. "It's not sports, grades . . . you start thinking about it when you're ten, and you don't stop until the day you die."

Yes, nothing was more important than scoring. All the girls of the world were evenly divided into Those Who Wouldn't and Those Who Would, and the important moral and philosophical questions that the boys spent their time discussing were: How far would Those Who Would go (these boys weren't merely interested in copping some quick feels) and how one might (in the most gentlemanly manner possible short of actual abduction) persuade Those Who Wouldn't to enter the ranks of Those Who Would.

John had just gotten his license when he had a shot at his high school dream date. She was one of those girls who was so pretty that it hurt; she already had a boyfriend but had relented at John's invitation. The plan: Take her to the drive-in in the good old Ford Galaxy and go, team, go!—one night of glory. John had no doubt whatsoever that once she came into contact with his potent sexual aura, well, she would be a goner, his forever, putty in his hands. "He picked her up and took her skating at his Uncle Joe's," Ripley says, picking up the story. "When they got in the car to leave, John backed right into another car. He gets out, embarrassed as hell, assesses the damage, exchanges information with the driver, apologizes, and then parks at Hook's for a pack of cigarettes. He gets back in, puts the car in Reverse, and *wham!*— yep, right into another car. So he had to do the same deal with the driver of the other car, right? They finally arrive at the drive-in, park, and John pounces. I mean, he was kissing her as if his life depended on it! Within minutes, he had her skirt up over her head, and in his overheated mind he's figuring, *Ah-ha, I've got her now!*—when all of a sudden, the lights come on: 'That ends

"I'd sit outside strumming my guitar and wait for the girls to come by . . ."

tonight's presentation, ladies and gentlemen . . .' It just didn't work out for him."

Not everybody remembers him as so forward, however. "He liked to talk big and make you think he was tough," Margaret Jones Nierman, one of his very first girlfriends, recalled for the 1984 Cinemax documentary, "but when you got to know him you realized how nice he was, and really very sensitive . . ."

John Mellencamp did his best to hide this part of himself. "When I was in high school, girls who liked you always sat close to you in cars, and it always bummed me out. If a girl got in the car and sat close to me I'd tell her to get away from me—it didn't look cool. I was worried about what other people thought. When you grow up, you realize that when you see a guy walking down the street hand-in-hand with a girl, you can make fun of it, but the deep-down, dark secret is that you're not only making fun of him but you're making fun of yourself. Because under the same circumstances, you would do the same thing. If I'd known the truth, the girl would have been sitting next to me the whole time . . ."

Still, by the standards of the times, John Mellencamp was a sexually precocious young man, having lost his virginity at the age of fourteen. He spent his teen years exactly like most of his friends, in a nearly perpetual state of unrelieved semi-tumescence, cruising Seymour and all the neighboring towns, driving a length of the Interstate that stretched for hundreds of miles, dreaming of finding that one girl—a girl like Melissa! One hour's drive up to Indianapolis was the place that John called "heaven on earth," the Whiteland Barn—a huge place, two floors of dancing and fun, with thousands of kids with rolled-up pants kicking to James Brown, with hamburgers and fries, and with bands like the Box Tops and the Strawberry Alarm Clock. One night she suddenly appeared, petite and fetching, with beautiful ass-length brown hair that had one rebellious streak of peroxide cascading down off her head like a beacon of sin. Melissa was every Indiana boy's wet dream of a trashy high school girl, impossibly cool, the best dancer at the barn—but wild, a girl from Shelbyville who was clearly from the wrong side of the tracks. She even had a little tattoo in a very private place! John gave her his class ring and even brought her home to meet his parents, who hated her—"She told Mom to get fucked"—which endeared her to John even more, but the relationship petered out. Still, today the mere mention of Melissa causes John to wax nostalgic to the point of rhapsody. "She was," he says simply, "the It Girl of my life."

After Melissa, it was business as usual, scouring the town for girls, dreaming of blonde Playmates of the Month and California beach bunnies.

They'd cruise out in Dr. Ripley's big Oldsmobile to pick up girls and bring them out to Cypress Lake to park, but most of the time the girls were so homely that the boys would be laughing too hard to go through with anything. After one such encounter, Mark and John dropped off two girls, and Ripley, scratching his head in dismay, said, "Man, I *swear* that girl I was with was wearing a jock! I stuck my hands down her pants and I felt this little strap . . ."

"Ripley, you idiot," John howled, "that was no jock—that was a Kotex belt!"

Sad, very sad . . .

Of course, when the fair came to Jackson County, you could go out to the hoot-show tent and sit around with a bunch of farmers watching Princess Tanyka perform such astonishing feats as smoking cigarettes vaginally and picking up Coke bottles in the same manner. And then there was good old Handy, a bespectacled wallflower of a girl with a legendary propensity to perform what Kinsey described as "manual manipulation of the penis to orgasm," sometimes under a table in the school library (hence her nickname).

"He thought he was Bob Bitchen in high school. He thought he could pick up any chick in town!"

Finally, during his junior year in high school, John Mellencamp fell in love. He met Priscilla Esterline one night when he and his rowdy friends had sneaked out of their houses after curfew and crashed a party in town. "I heard this guy talking loud," Cil says, "acting real tough. He was really cute though."

Cil Esterline was three years older than John, with a job and an apartment of her own—a down-to-earth, easygoing girl with lazy brown eyes and chestnut hair that she wore pinned on top of her head, with strands falling wispily down her alabaster neck. Within about two months they were dating steadily, exploring the world together in a sweet haze of marijuana smoke. "We were together all the time," John says. "The thing I loved about our relationship was that she became like my best friend. We did LSD together for the first time. Cil wasn't afraid to get on the back of a motorcycle and go a hundred miles per hour . . ."

Moreover, she provided still another vehicle for John's ongoing revolt: His parents didn't approve of her.

Marilyn and Richard Mellencamp were a textbook case of American parents who simply did not cope well with the transformations of the 1960s—with hippies, pot smoking, long hair, student protest, the sexual revolution—with the very things that John was doing as his senior year rolled around. Not only was John hanging around this older girl named Cil, but he was spending time with older guys like Gary Boebinger, the fellow John used to throw rocks at from the front lawn, who had grown into a bearded, long-haired, left-leaning high school English teacher. Marilyn worried that "Bo" was feeding her son all kinds of spurious, subversive notions. "Boebinger was an influence on John," she recognizes. "He'd come over here and give us all this static about how pretentious we were. You know, 'What do you need a *fur coat* for?' I'd get mad because we'd started from ground zero and worked for all the 'stuff' he was putting down. It was galling to have worked so hard to create a better life for your kid, and then one day he comes home with long hair and sees you as some redneck who doesn't know what it's *about*. Of course, John never called Richard a redneck—he wouldn't have lived to tell the tale."

To them, John was turning into a walking advertisement for everything that was going wrong with the nation. Little by little, inch by inch, his hair was sneaking down over his ears—a public flouting of his father's authority that oftentimes led to actual combat. To John, the fact that he was the first in his class to grow his hair long was a badge of honor. "He was always the first to relay the news to the rest of the kids," says Gary Boebinger. "They all kind of looked to him to see if he could get away with it." This bold-faced effrontery was only compounded by his smoking of marijuana, while riding around the town—he stayed away from home as much as possible. When he did come home, he'd go directly upstairs, close his door, and play acid rock at an ear-splitting decibel level until somebody pounded on his door and threatened him with bodily harm.

The growing antagonism came to a head over the diet pills scandal. Mark Ripley had been shedding pounds with the help of an amphetamine prescription and had given his buddy John a little stash of the pills for his own recreational purposes. One evening, John mistakenly took a few too many uppers and spent the entire night rolling around in his bed, sweating, wide-eyed with anxiety. The next day, he looked so horrible in class that a teacher sent him to the office for "behaving strangely"; school officials, suspicious of the pale, bug-eyed, dry-mouthed, shaking figure before them, decided to search Ripley's Volkswagen. When they opened the door, Ripley's entire cache of pills came spilling out onto the pavement. Then things got ugly: Ripley was hauled out of class and the police came to interrogate the boys and make dire threats. As it turned out, the cops didn't prosecute them, but the boys decided that they'd better tell their parents just in case. "They had a fit," John says. "That's when the old man decided he was finally going to try and straighten me out."

Richard Mellencamp had reached the breaking point with his son. "He came and got John out of school and ripped the leather bracelet off his arm and punched him around some," Ripley remembers. "I saw John after he got back. He was bummed out. His hair was all cut off and he was wearing a new pair of pants." There wasn't much John could do except for one little gesture of defiance calculated to irritate the old man: He left the house with a makeshift sign around his neck that read I AM THE PRODUCT OF MY FATHER!

As if this weren't trouble enough, several occasions of careless contraception had boomeranged, and Cil was pregnant. She wasn't about to get an abortion; and John, stoned, blissfully in love as only a seventeen-year-old high school senior could be, was determined to "do the right thing." He decided to let Cil sound out his mother on the subject, so one afternoon, Cil came over to the house for a heart-to-heart with Marilyn Mellencamp. Sitting together in the dining room, Cil asked, "How would you feel if John and I decided to get married?"

"Don't even talk about it because John's *not* going to marry you," was Marilyn's shocked response. "I would *never* consent to it! He's not prepared

Yearbook photo, Seymour High, Class of 1970.

to get married for a long time—he's still a *kid*. And you're not the girl he should marry anyway . . .''

Tears were streaming down Cil's face by the end of the conversation. The words were cruel enough; Marilyn had no idea that Cil was already two months pregnant.

One day after school, toward the end of his senior year, Cil picked John up and they drove across the state line to Louisville, where there was no age of consent. The week before, they'd gone down there for the blood test, and, like a bad omen, the needle had broken off in John's arm. "He almost passed out, right on the spot,'' Cil recalls. They had no witnesses except a local cop and the secretary in the office of the Justice of the Peace. When it was over, they drove back, and Cil dropped off John at his parents' house—as if nothing had really happened. After all, says John: "Neither of us had any idea what the fuck we were going to do!''

As it turned out, word got out very quickly. "We were at the after-prom party,'' Cil says, "and a bunch of kids came up to us and said, 'Congratulations!' They read a notice in the *Louisville Courier-Journal* that we'd gotten married. John almost fell on the floor—his father got that paper at his office.''

Panic-stricken, John called his brother Joe in Bloomington for advice.

"You've got to tell Mom and Dad," Joe told him, "but if I were you, I'd have Grandma Laura do it for you!"

"He and Cil came over that Saturday morning," recalls Laura Mellencamp, "and they told me and my husband. I said, 'Just sit down and we'll have breakfast.' John was so nervous his shirt was wet all down his arms: 'Dad's gonna beat the hell out of me!' I called Richard and said, 'Come on over here—we've got a little surprise for you. Only one thing: Don't bring Marilyn, okay?' "

Marilyn was furious—the *nerve* of them to bar her from a family gathering—and sat seething in the car while Richard went inside and was duly informed about the marriage and pregnancy. John had been right about at least one part of his strategy: Being at Grandma's precluded the possibility of his father putting his head through the nearest wall. "Richard just gave him a real dirty look," Grandma Laura says. "The first thing he said was, 'Let me see the certificate!' Then he left . . ."

"Well, I'll just go up to an attorney and have it annulled," Marilyn said calmly, upon hearing the news. "He's still a resident of Indiana, and he's still in high school. There's no way . . ."

John had to intercede personally with his mother to prevent the annulment of the marriage. "Please, Mom, I wish you wouldn't do this," he begged her. After much cajoling and handwringing, she finally relented. "He really believed he needed her," Marilyn says today. "To me it seemed like she'd brainwashed him. But if that was what he wanted . . ."

To Marilyn, Cil Esterline had snatched her son from the very bosom of the family, and she resented her new daughter-in-law bitterly. Things weren't much better between John and Richard. "Dad and I didn't talk to each other for over a year after that," John relates. But their more pressing problem was where to go? Cil had a job as a telephone operator, but John was an unemployed high school graduate with a bad reputation and long hair. For a while, they moved in with Bo and his wife, Donna, then settled in a trailer park in Vallonia, along the White River. "At ten dollars a month, it was overpriced," Cil says. "There was no running water, and we slept on the dining room table . . ." Their next stop was a small apartment in the back of Mark Ripley's grandmother's house. That didn't last long, either: The old lady grew tired of seeing John's cigarette butts all over the front porch and gave them the boot. In the end, they had no choice but to move in with Cil's parents, the Esterlines.

Michelle Mellencamp was born December 4, 1970. Her father, at first afraid to hold her, was soon throwing her gleefully up in the air and catching her like

To his parents, John was turning into "a walking advertisement for everything that was going wrong with the nation."

a football, giving everybody a heart attack. While Cil went back to her job, John's life consisted of "staying home, playing Frisbee in the morning, going out and sitting on the hood of a car in the afternoon, smoking cigarettes, doing dope, going home, eating dinner, listening to records at night." What about his job? "I had a job as an electrician's helper for a while but I couldn't handle it. There was no way I was going to work. I was into drugs . . ."

After eighteen months of freeloading, the Esterlines, who'd provided them with room and board and gas money and even tickets to rock concerts, finally gave them the heave-ho. "I was fucking around with rock bands," John told Chris Connelly of *Rolling Stone* in 1982, recalling this period of his life. "Their attitude was, 'You ain't never gonna do anything with rock & roll.' It was like, 'Hey, I've *only* been living off you for a year and a half! Hey, another ten, fifteen years!' "

The necessity of getting a job was forestalled for another couple of years when John got accepted to Vincennes University, a two-year college not far from Seymour. "With my bad academic record," John says, "that was just about the only school hard up enough to take me! I figured I'd just go down there and lay around." He packed up Cil and Michelle and moved into a small house with his old friend Tim Elsner, enrolling as a communications major. "In those days he wanted to be a DJ," Elsner recalls. "He thought all they had to do was sit around and play records, and he was really into rock and roll. Our whole living room was wall-to-wall rock posters—not one square inch of white space—with black drapes and black lights. You'd be in there midday and it'd be pitch black . . .''

The living room may have looked like the typical psychedelic den of iniquity, but John Mellencamp was already well past his drug days. "He hated drugs in college," Elsner says. "Back in Seymour, when it was unheard of, he was doing it before everybody else, but he outgrew it. Having Michelle had something to do with it." "I was tired of the whole hippie thing," John relates, "the drugs, the philosophy. Everybody had long hair and I got sick of that. It seemed such a hoax, because we all believed we were going to change the world. Material things weren't going to matter anymore, that whole bill of rights. All the sixties did was enable guys to wear blue jeans to work. Smoke marijuana, sit around drinking beer. It was a waste of time . . ."

Whereas John had once thrilled to the flowery sounds of Donovan and John Sebastian, now he only wanted to listen to Iggy Pop, the New York Dolls, and especially David Bowie—nihilistic, decadent street punks who wore makeup and nail polish and did outrageous things—androgynes, drag queens, true rock & roll flotsam and jetsam. The Next Big Thing had arrived in his life: Glitter Rock. He cut his hair into a shag, sent away for a pair of outrageously high platform shoes, started acquiring the accoutrements of glitter and experimenting with "the look," all the while playing Iggy Pop's "Search and Destroy," and Bowie's *Ziggy Stardust* nonstop.

John, Cil, and 'Chelle, summer of 1971.

At radio station WVTU, where John took a night stint on the air for credit in one of his broadcasting courses, he delighted in exposing his listeners to the new music he had discovered; but it was rapidly becoming clear that he didn't have much of a future in the field. As Tim Elsner explains: "He was great spinning the records, but then it would come time to rip the paper out of the teletype machine and do the newscast. Then, he was a goner. He was—and still is—the worst in the world at reading aloud. Of course, the Vietnam war was still going on, and he'd be stumbling along and then he'd come to some Asiatic names and get completely confounded and start cussing on the air—'Ho, ho,—*oh, fuck*—Ho Chi Minh!' He became something of a legend among the kids in the school because he had the reputation of a cutup, and they thought he was doing it on purpose. People started tuning him in, figuring, this has *got* to be an act—nobody can *really* be that bad!"

John managed to limp through his courses by applying the absolute minimum of time and effort and somehow sweet-talking his professors into giving him passing grades. He passed his sociology final—a lengthy, multiple choice affair—by cheating, with the help of his reliable old friend, Elsner. "We devised this complicated system of hand signals and coughs," Elsner reveals, "and John kept falling behind. By question number thirty, he started getting mad: 'Goddammit, I'm only on twenty-eight!' The teaching assistants all started getting suspicious. "Goddammit, Elsner, don't go so fast!' He was crazy . . .I don't know how he did it, but he ended up getting a B."

When John wasn't in school or listening to music, most of his time was devoted to indulging his prankish sense of humor. Tim Elsner recalled a typical incident: "Ted lived behind us in this converted garage apartment, and we took showers at his house because we only had a tub. Anyway, this guy named Wizard had the apartment next to Ted's and their showers were adjoining, separated by this wall. John had a feud going with him because he thought Wizard was giving Cil the eye. When Wizard's girlfriend came to visit, John decided that he was going to peep through this crack in the wall and watch them take a shower together. But the crack wasn't big enough, so John takes a broom handle and tries to gingerly enlarge the hole while they're showering. Of course, John never did anything 'gingerly' in his life: He tried to force the thing, and it went shooting through the wall, right into Wizard's head! The girl is standing there screaming and John casually says through the hole, 'Oh, *sorry*, I didn't mean to *do* that . . .' "

Toward the end of college, John once again became interested in playing in a rock band. The result was Trash, Indiana's notorious, shortlived, but only legitimate glitter rock act. "We were all horrible, but I was good enough to play guitar for what John wanted to do," says Larry Crane. "Plus, I was young, which made it easy for him to boss me around."

Larry Crane was Seymour's guitar whiz, a natural musician almost five years younger than John, who could play by ear just about any song ever written. (Awed by Crane's ability, John knew a good thing when he saw it—Larry remains his guitarist to this day.) Along with Cil's brother, Dennis Esterline, they started playing music that, to unfamiliar ears, must have sounded like it was from outer space. "Not many people out here were listening to that kind of music," Crane says. "I remember one gig we had in a theater up in Indianapolis. We did Free's 'Walkin' My Shadow' with just the guitar and bass, and then the rest of the band would come out and we'd do Iggy's 'I Wanna Be Your Dog,'' Bowie's 'Suffragette City' and 'Ziggy,' and then some stuff John had written, which never went over too well. Someone chucked a bottle which went skipping across the stage, and I just said, *'Oh, no.'* " "We certainly didn't work much," John laughs. "We were into the Bowie look, but Bowie was too dressed up for us. Our look was more greasy, more Mexican. We had those little doodads of hair hanging underneath our lips and we wore heavy makeup and my hair was dyed pink or yellow or something . . ."

To fully appreciate the sight of Trash in full glitter regalia, one must imagine the reactions of people on the streets in 1973 as they went prancing by in their high-heeled boots and mink collars. Looking at photos of the band today, John Mellencamp just shakes his head in disbelief and mutters, "Fuck, no wonder my parents *hated* me . . ." "We wanted to stand out and look different," notes Ted Mellencamp, then also attending Vincennes and serving as the band's "road manager." "If I saw a guy dressed like we did today I'd think he was definitely queer. Trash was the worst band in the world. Even the guys in the band hated it."

"Hey, the plain fact was that it was *dangerous* looking like that," exclaims Larry Crane. "One night after this gig, we went into this truckstop to eat something while Ted parked the van, and these truckers were staring a hole through us like they were going to take us apart. John was getting real paranoid, and just then Ted walks in. At the time Ted looked exactly like Lou Reed on the *Sally Can't Dance* album cover: black leather, short platinum-blond hair, sunglasses on even if it was pitch dark. 'Ted,' John whispers to him, 'let's get the hell out of here—some sonofabitch is saying stuff about me,' and Ted whips around and says, 'Which sonofabitch—this one *here?*' and points out some giant! We were cringing with terror but he backed the whole place down. They thought he was *armed*."

Trash didn't last too long after graduation. It was time for John Mellencamp to get serious. With a wife and child, he did not have the luxury of procrastination, of lying around and figuring out what he wanted to do with his life. He needed a job—fast. "I interviewed for one job with a radio station," he says, "a young station run by old men. The job would have been to have dinner with prospective advertisers, flirt with their wives, present the right 'image'. It was the first job I ever applied for in the conventional business world—and the last."

He moved his family back to Seymour, into a concrete garage on Thirteenth Street that had been converted into a two-bedroom apartment and took a job installing telephones instead.

As John settled into the stifling routine of his job, music began to matter to him more and more. With all the extra money that was left over after their bills were paid, he usually made a beeline for the record bins. He also started playing more often and tried to write his own music. "He'd sit around making up songs," Cil recalls. "He had this autoharp and this Hummingbird that we'd gotten him on credit. Then he got a Gibson Dove later on . . ." "He'd be sitting on top of a picnic bench at Star Hollow Beach," Ripley says, "strumming a Dylan tune or making up a song, and I'd think, *Damn,* that's pretty good—that could make it on the radio." Unfortunately, he could never quite figure what he wanted to write *about,* so he started trying to write songs with an ex-classmate named George Green. "John was always introducing me to music," Green says. "Our tastes were different—he called the music I liked 'wimp rock.' He'd play me a Bowie song and say, 'Let's write something like *that.'* None of the stuff we wrote was any good. I remember one song we wrote called 'Loser,' a real derogatory song about Lou Reed." Green pauses, laughs. "No wonder it stunk . . . What business did two guys in Seymour have writing a song about *Lou Reed?"*

Around this time, he got a job playing at the Chatterbox, an old red-brick bar off Second Street in Seymour. The manager of the place hoped some live music would bring in a younger clientele, and considering that the only people who ever went to the Chatterbox were the old alcoholics of the town, anyone under the age of seventy would have represented a younger crowd. John's four appearances at the little bar made him something of a local celebrity, and he began to realize how much he enjoyed performing. "It was like a big party when he played," Ripley says. "There was cheap beer and he got the guy to set up a little stage and he got Ted to string some lights. He'd sit up there and entertain you for hours . . ."

At the same time, the drudgery of his nine-to-five life began to weigh him

Trash! Left to right are Larry Crane, Dennis Esterline, John J. Mellencamp, and Kevin Wissing.

down. "He was unhappy and under pressure," Cil recognizes. "He knew he wanted more out of life than what he had, that he'd have to do something. I used to get angry with him sometimes—hey, you know, *I* work, too—you're not the only one who gets depressed around here!"

What drove John Mellencamp to the notion of making a record? Certainly, the most naïve fantasies of the rock & roll life-style and what it was all about were at the very root of the dream. "My dad always told me, 'Son, you'll never be able to find a job where you can sit back, prop your feet up, listen to records, and drink Big Red.' It's funny, but I wanted to figure out how I could do that, and the only things I'd ever been good at were showing off and singing. And everybody kept saying, 'You got a wife and kid—when are you going to take on some responsibility?' Then I decided I was going to cut a record! Everybody said, 'John, wake up. People from Seymour don't make *records*. They work in the fields and they work in the factories, and if you're lucky, you can be like your old man. Get a good job by the time you're fifty and that's that!' That's what made me really want to go out and do it— everyone saying *you can't.''*

John couldn't get the thought out of his mind, and yet the more he talked about it, the more people ridiculed the notion. "I became obsessed with the idea," he says. "So I started trying to make demos, sending them off to the record companies." "He had the entire wall of his apartment completely decorated with the rejection letters," recalls Dave Knotts. "I thought it was nice that he was trying, but it didn't seem like he had a chance in hell of making it." "I'll tell you something," relates Gary Boebinger, "he was *serious* from ground level zero. I remember having a discussion with him one day, and he asked me, "Bo, how do you see yourself in the future?' I said, 'Just some guy living here, teaching.' He said, 'See, that's the difference. I see myself as a *rock star.' ''*

The more serious he became about music, the less serious he was about his job. Indeed, his rounds for the phone company began to resemble episodes of "The Three Stooges," with Moe, Larry, and Curly all rolled into one package; he once managed to cross the wrong wires at a waystation and disconnect all the phones of Freetown, Indiana. Eventually, his long-suffering superiors began to lose patience. "I swear a lot and I'm kind of vulgar sometimes," he would cheerfully admit to Lynn Van Matre of the *Chicago Tribune* in 1979. "I'd go into a house to install a phone, and when the thing wouldn't work right, I'd start banging on it, cursing. I guess it upset the housewives, because they started calling up the phone company to complain."

"I was working at a grocery store and John came in one day and told me he'd been fired from his job with the phone company," Ted Mellencamp remembers. "Hell, I thought that was the worst thing that could have happened—he had a wife and a kid and, you know, you've gotta eat! He looked at me and smiled and said, 'I can't believe it took them so long—I've been tryin' for months!' That was the first I heard about his plan to go to New York and become a songwriter and an entertainer."

Marilyn Mellencamp certainly wasn't about to encourage a trip to New York—John's older brother, Joe, who also played music, had almost made a mockery of his life by trying to succeed with a group called Pure Jam. But she nonetheless realized there was nothing she could do: "I knew he'd have to go to New York sooner or later to get it out of his system."

With several months unemployment benefits saved, John packed some clothes, his guitar, and Cil into his Ford and headed for the big city, knowing nothing about the economic realities of the business, nothing about recording or promotion, with only a couple of songs under his belt. "That kind of stuff never entered my mind. I wanted to make a record that went on a piece of plastic. That was it."

It took them eighteen straight hours to reach New York City. They arrived just as the sun was coming up over the Manhattan skyline. "The first thing we saw when we got to town was some hooker beating up a john. I was scared to death! We booked into the Holiday Inn downtown and I just bolted the door for twelve hours—wouldn't go anywhere. I said to Cil, 'Fuck, I don't know if I wanna do this that bad!' "

Before long, they ventured out like timid little animals. Soon, John was making his rounds, which consisted in putting in personal appearances at all the record companies that had rejected his tape. The sight of him stepping off elevators would strike terror in the hearts of receptionists, not to mention the A&R people he would accost and harass on their way in and out of offices.

After two weeks, with his money just about gone, John found his way up to Sunshine Records, a small, independent label located in the Gulf & Western Building. The doors were unguarded by any receptionist so he just strolled in, encountering a fellow in A&R. John introduced himself and played his tape—it never occurred to him that the "producer" was merely a shady lawyer using someone else's office during the lunch hour. "Well," John asked anxiously, "whaddya think?"

"Not bad. The tape stinks though. No wonder you haven't been able to get a deal. Tell you what: You get two grand and I'll kick in two grand and we'll cut you another demo tape. Then I'll get you a good deal, no problem."

John was ecstatic; it was the first positive response to his music from anybody in New York. They shook hands on the deal, and John hurried back to the hotel to tell Cil that he was going to be a star. But where could he get $2,000? His first stop was Richard Mellencamp, who told him, "Nothing doing, son. It all sounds a bit dicey to me." However John managed to persuade his father at least to cosign a bank loan. He wired the money and traveled to the city again, this time to a small sixteen-track studio to make a demo tape of "Kicks," the old Paul Revere and the Raiders song. "I'll call you in a few weeks when I have a deal put together. Don't worry, I've got great connections," John was told. He went home and waited for a call that never came. Three, four, five weeks passed; he called New York every day, running up astronomical phone bills. Nothing. "Then I finally realized what had happened," John says ruefully. "He'd taken my money, put a thousand into the tape, and the rest probably went up his girlfriend's nose. You know, I

The photo that John was sending out with his demos, which attracted attention at MainMan.
The beatnik in the background is George Green.

was just some kid from Indiana. This was my first taste of the record business."

Months of low spirits followed, during which both friends and family counseled him to give up the dream. "There were times I told him, 'Man, why don't you quit this rock and roll bullshit and just get a regular job,' " Ripley admits. " 'Your wife's supporting you and she ain't making enough money and you got a kid and you're spending five hundred bucks a month on phone bills to New York! Ask them to take you back at the phone company.' But he had the most singleminded kind of determination. Thank God he didn't listen to me."

John decided to travel back to the city still another time to track down his demo of "Kicks"—but this time he had another plan. Instead of trying to shop himself to a record company, where he didn't really know the ropes, he'd find himself a slick manager, someone who had all the contacts and knew every little nuance of the music business. So, why not somebody with a high profile? Being the sort who always read the backs of albums, John knew that one of his idols, David Bowie, was managed by Tony DeFries; and, being an avid reader of *Rolling Stone,* he'd learned that Bowie and DeFries were on the outs and that DeFries was looking for new talent. He had already sent MainMan, DeFries's management company, a tape along with a photo of himself dolled up in a three-piece suit seated in a wing chair. Now he decided to drop by in person.

He arrived at the MainMan office on the last day of 1975, starving and down to his last few dollars. He found himself in a roomful of Bowie clones, all clutching their little demo tapes, all waiting to be discovered. With his frayed denims and ducktail, he looked like quite the oddball in that antechamber full of glam rockers, and it wasn't long before he attracted the attention of one of DeFries's assistants, Mary Carol Culligan. "Where are you from?" she asked, noticing his accent. "Indiana," he said. "You're kidding, so am I!" she exclaimed. "What the hell are you doing *here?*"

John handed her the tape, and she took down his name and number; he thought nothing of it and left the building, only to find that his car had been towed from the parking spot. "That was the lowest day of my life,' " he remembers. "I'd been staying down in this scrummy little apartment, and I figured, well, this just ain't making it. I got my car out of hock and just left town . . ."

Driving home, he couldn't quite bring himself to admit that he'd been defeated—almost two years had elapsed since he'd set out to make a record. There was one possibility left—a dippy little independent record label in

Louisville that he'd heard about, so he detoured down into Kentucky, found the place, and played his tape. The two men who owned the company just grimaced and shook their heads mournfully. "Naw, sorry . . ."

"Well, what the hell's wrong with it?" John asked petulantly. "What makes this any worse than anything else you've got?"

"Well, if you must know—it *sucks*," was their undiplomatic response.

Well, enough said; at least he'd really tried. Now he'd just have to find a real job—the thought weighed on his chest like a cold stone. He pulled into the driveway, and no sooner had he kissed Cil than the phone started ringing. He picked it up.

"Jawn?" The voice was deep, British.

"Yeah?"

"Tony DeFries . . . I've been trying to track you down. Why did you leave town so fast? Listen, I heard your tape and I think we can do business."

"Great," John said, trying his best to sound nonchalant.

"Why don't you come back to New York as soon as you can—"

"Because I don't have any goddamn money left," John told him.

DeFries laughed. "I'll send you a plane ticket first thing tomorrow . . ."

The cabbie who picked him up at the airport was a wizened old fellow. John gave him the MainMan address and settled in the back of the cab, still stunned by his good fortune. The cabbie asked, "Where you from?"

"Indiana," was John's half-proud, half-embarrassed reply.

"Yeah? Whatcha doin' here?"

"I'm gonna m-m-m-make a record!" In his excitement, his childhood stutter had returned.

The cabbie turned and gave him the once-over. "How old are you?"

"Twenty-four."

The cabbie glanced at his face in the rear-view mirror. "Son," he said with paternal concern, "do yourself a favor and go on back home before you get *hurt*."

John paid him no mind, but as the city skyline came slowly into view, his heart began to pound like a pneumatic drill.

II

SERIOUS BUSINESS

Wherein a Star Blooms amid the Indiana Corn

Didn't know what you were getting into
When you walked into this room, now did you, kid . . .
—"Serious Business"

Tony DeFries, a large, ursine Englishman who usually had an expensive cigar jutting out of his heavily bearded face, had two portraits hanging in his plush Central Park South office that should have told John Mellencamp something about his whole approach to the music business. The first was of Colonel Tom Parker, the legendary carny barker who had guided a poor boy from East Tupelo, Mississippi, named Elvis Presley to fame, fortune, and (many say) ruin; the other was P. T. Barnum, the father of the American circus, "the greatest showman in the world," and the man who had been one of the Colonel's inspirations. Both of DeFries's idols had the following in common: They were wildly successful businessmen who had amassed vast fortunes selling their respective products to the American public; and both, in their heart of hearts, were illusionists, con men, grifters who believed that the demand for their products had more to do with image and promotion than with actual substance. Unbeknownst to John Mellencamp as he sat there getting to know DeFries, he was being sized up as The Next Big Thing by one of the master image-mongers of the music business—a hard-nosed, manipulative salesman notorious for arrogance, ruthless deal-making, endless lawsuits, extravagant hype, and megadollar success.

DeFries began his career as a poor Jewish boy in London and, by all accounts, determined at a young age to raise himself to a position of prestige and wealth. He became a successful solicitor/businessman while still relatively young and made his way into the music business during the 1960s by hooking up with producer Mickey Most and handling the affairs of Eric Burdon and the Animals. Like John Mellencamp, David Bowie, né Jones, was only twenty-four when he first found DeFries and asked him for help in getting out of his management deal with Kenneth Pitt. In Bowie, DeFries found his perfect product—he would play Colonel Parker to Bowie's ascending Elvis with devastating effectiveness, presiding haughtily over one of the greatest musical phenomena of the 1970s. As Bowie swept England, transforming himself from album to album into the sulky drag queen of *The Man Who Sold the World,* into the gender-smashing androgyne of *Hunky Dory,* and then into the space-suited moonrocker of *The Rise and Fall of Ziggy Stardust and the Spiders from Mars,* DeFries force-fed each new image to press and public through his new company, MainMan. At MainMan's zenith in 1974, as Bowie conquered America on his huge *Diamond Dogs* tour, with its herculean props (an enormous, surreal cityscape complete with catwalks), DeFries had an army of sixty people working for him; a stable of talent that included Iggy Pop, Lou Reed, and Mott the Hoople; and a reputation as the unchallenged impresario of glitter rock. The American record industry viewed him with guarded awe after he negotiated Bowie's original contract with RCA, which is said to have been "re-defined" or increased fourfold by DeFries before the first option came due. The press, on the other hand, despised him: DeFries's aloofness and insulting attitude always implied that he regarded them as a bunch of ink-stained wretches who could be made to jump through hoops like everybody else, to be used at will for the promotion of his product. Hence his industrywide nickname, "Tony DeepFreeze."

December 25, 1974—the day Bowie decided to leave MainMan—had been a red-letter day in the life of Tony DeFries. Bowie had wanted more control over his career and was sliding further and further into isolation, paranoia, and heavy drugs. The split was an acrimonious one, ending in a flurry of lawsuits and injunctions that would tie up Bowie's money in escrow for an eternity. DeFries was on the look-out for somebody to take Bowie's place—some raw talent he could mold into his next superstar. He felt that he had "made" David Bowie; he could easily make others.

The MainMan staff was an interesting collection of human specimens. The late Jamie Andrews, for instance, had begun his career as a photographer and then became an actor who cut his teeth on the Theater of the Ridiculous and on the crazed plays of Jackie Curtis at New York's LaMama. Andrews served as Bowie's link with Manhattan's theatrical avant-garde and the visual arts/high fashion scene. Other colorful types, too, became part of the organization—among them Cherry Vanilla and Wayne County—making MainMan seem like quite a bizarre menagerie to the outside world.

And so, into this den of wolves, fops, zany transvestites, weirdos, egomaniacs, and flashy, fast-talking music business types walked John Mellencamp of Seymour, Indiana.

"Now, Jawn," DeFries said at the end of their meeting, "you must trust me that I know what's best for you and do exactly as I say, do you understand?"

John blinked and nodded.

"Good, then we have a deal. You'll be a *big* star in a year's time."

They shook hands, and a young man with a rather long track record of never listening to what people told him to do found himself placing his fate in the hands of another.

"The deal was that I was working for the company," explains John. "It was a five-year contract. There was no discussion of points or anything; I never even had an attorney. I signed a piece of paper on his say-so—I liked him. Nothing was ever explained to me, and even if it had been, I wouldn't have understood. Looking back, I can't believe how naïve I was, but at the time, it was all like a dream coming true. I was obsessed with getting a record deal, with making a record. And if DeFries could help me do it—hey, whatever it takes. What did I know about it?"

The MainMan plan was a simple one. "We felt that there was a whole revival of small-town Americanism going on," Jamie Andrews says. "The image would be of an all-American boy, kind of 1950s, like Elvis or James Dean. John certainly had the *look*. The idea was to make him a star in Indiana first, then bring him out of the Midwest, à la Ted Nugent." The angle of promotion was best summed up in the lead sentence of John's MainMan biography: *Johnny Cougar is a rock singer, a small midwestern town, and a way of life all thrown into one.* "He reminds me of an early Elvis," DeFries began telling people in the business and in the press. "He's so American—the most American artist I've seen since Dylan—and I think he'll capture the same kind of thing Dylan did." The MainMan hypemobile machinery was being retooled. Instead of glam rock, or rock and rouge, it was getting ready to manufacture rock populism, USA-style. Of course, the music business, used to the most shameless hype campaigns, paid DeFries's newest "discovery" little mind at first, but when he started stoking the embers of legends like Dylan and Elvis, interest was naturally piqued. Word began to spread that Tony had found a "new boy" and was grooming The Next Big Thing.

The package, as MainMan viewed it, would be a fairly easy one to put together. "We knew instinctively that he was a brat," Andrews says of John, "but you could tell that his heart was in the right place. He had a distinctive voice that we felt had real potential for rock . . . Eventually, Tony decided to give him some money. He was big on that—make them stop doing what they were doing and concentrate. Tony felt that the whole thing could be done inexpensively. We decided to let John go ahead and do his demos in Indiana."

John later described his initial relationship with Tony DeFries in an interview with *Sounds* magazine: "He tried to father me and at first I played along . . . I wanted to make sure he liked me and I hated myself for it . . . His whole thing was, 'As long as Johnny's got a bit of money, he won't bitch.' "

As it turned out, DeFries's instincts about using money to control and mold John Mellencamp were right on target. "All I knew was the guy came in and paid my bills," relates John. "I was debt-free for the first time since I'd been married. He bought us a washer, a dryer, and was paying me about a thousand a month. I thought, Fuck, I'm rich! This is the rock and roll business!"

Things began to change with dizzying speed. DeFries thought it was undignified for John and Cil to be living in a garage. "You're moving," he informed them, and move they did—right into ex-Governor Whitcomb's summer home. "People couldn't believe it!" Cil says, laughing uproariously. "It was exciting! All of sudden we had this feeling that—all right, maybe we *can* do this and show all these people. I think I also began to feel threatened on some level: What's gonna happen to me and Michelle if it *does* happen?"

With his mind suddenly inflamed with a hundred new anxieties, John began to have trouble sleeping at night. After all, he wanted to do well, to really pull it off, and he'd only written a few songs for an album; having been a passionate aficionado of rock & roll, he knew what constituted good music and what was dross and drivel. Given his scant repertoire and experience, he began to feel like a writer who'd only published a poem or a short story being given a contract to write the Great American Novel—he was scared shitless. "One night he had a real bad anxiety attack," Cil confides. "He really thought he was having a heart attack. 'Call Grandma!' he kept saying. We took him to the hospital and the doctor explained what was happening and shot him up with ten milligrams of Valium."

"I never really realized until I had that anxiety attack what stress and unhappiness really were," John observes. "Up until then, I thought life was a bowl of cherries. I did what I wanted, I came and went whenever I felt like it. Money was not important, paying my bills was something I never thought about. All of a sudden, you realize that there's much more to it than that, and it becomes harder to be happy. You have to work at it . . ."

Hanging out on a familiar streetcorner, early MainMan days. *(JJC Andrews/MainMan)*

About that time, DeFries and several of his associates, Jamie included, descended on Seymour for a lengthy visit. Ted Mellencamp recalls the scene at his parents' house when the maestro first strode through the door. "It was like meeting God or somebody—it was a big deal. Mom and Dad really catered to him—I was amazed at that. He came in with all these weird fucking people from New York, throwing money around like you wouldn't believe. It was real culture shock!"

"His mother and father both thought John was going nowhere," Jamie Andrews says. "They thought he wasn't going to amount to anything and treated him like a joke. In Marilyn's eyes, he was just trying to follow in the footsteps of his big brother, Joe, who'd played in a rock band for a while. The old man wanted him to get a good job in the electrician business, and Marilyn was more concerned about golf and tennis and her house; she had a very laissez-faire attitude. Not one person, especially his own family, took him seriously! They couldn't believe that Tony was serious about him."

"They were a bunch of nuts, the most overbearing people I've ever met in my life," Marilyn says of the MainMan clan, "but I liked Tony. He seemed to know right where he wanted to go with John. He impressed me as brilliant—British and Jewish—but he could also be terribly rude, obstinate, and insulting, sitting up there in his ivory tower overlooking Central Park. I couldn't believe he was spending all this money on my kid!" DeFries stayed with the Mellencamps for nine weeks, moving in with his child and girlfriend; by the time he left Seymour, he had Marilyn Mellencamp eating right out of his hand. Cil Mellencamp wasn't quite so sure about him. "He was smooth and suave; he talked like he was always completely in control and you believed him, but I had a feeling there might be trouble between him and John."

Getting John a record deal with a major label proved to be much harder than winning over the Mellencamps. "We beat on every bloody door to get people to listen," Jamie recalls, "and we encountered nothing but resistance—except for MCA. God knows why . . .''

DeFries found a sympathetic ear in the form of Bob Davis, then working in both A&R and Legal at MCA, who for some reason agreed that John might indeed just be the Next Big Thing. "He got very passionate about John," Jamie continues. "It seemed as if he literally fell in love with him. MCA started to think he was going to be the Midwestern Bruce Springsteen."

When Davis persuaded chairman Lou Cook and president Mike Maitland that MCA would be making a big mistake if they passed on John, a deal was struck.

Actually, DeFries managed to finagle a package deal. Not only had he sold John Mellencamp but MCA was also getting another MainMan client: Mick Ronson, the blond-maned, reed-thin guitarist who had played the Spider to Bowie's Ziggy. Ronson had stayed on with MainMan after the falling out with Bowie, and because he had tracked the guitars on such Bowie classics as "Suffragette City," John actively sought him out as a friend and adviser. "I'd heard that the deal MainMan made for us was for about a million dollars," John says. "I would ask them about the amount but I was always put off, and Mick didn't know either. Ronson really tried to teach me whatever he knew about the business, but the fact was he didn't know that much either! He was just another kid playing rock and roll . . ."

Mellencamp quickly developed a reputation as a cocky kid at the record company. In fact, during his first meeting with Lou Cook, the chief operating

officer of the label, John almost managed to sabotage the whole deal when he told him to "get fucked." "John was only reacting to some typical corporate music business rhetoric," recalls Jamie Andrews. "From the very beginning, he didn't like dealing with the 'suits,' as he called the businessmen of the industry. Cook was offended, though; the contract went through only after John apologized to him."

"I still almost couldn't believe it," says John. "With only a few lousy demos under my belt, I was signed to MCA! Now all I had to do was put an album together . . ."

The band that John put together, called the Tiger Force Band, consisted of Indiana musicians. First, he managed to track down Larry Crane, who'd left town to go off on the road with a country band, and tapped another local guitarist named Dave Parman, a high-strung, starstruck kid who'd played around town with John in bands like the Mason Brothers, who also had a knack for arrangement. Added to the roster were Wayne Hall on sax and Tom "Bub" Wince, a chubby, bull-necked fellow with a light, mellow touch on the piano. They lacked a steady drummer, not to mention consistency of style, direction; what they all had in common was that none of them had the slightest idea of what they were doing. With the $7,000 fronted by DeFries, they booked a small sixteen-track studio in Bloomington called Gilfoy, used mostly by classical and jazz musicians from the music department at Indiana University. "It took two weeks!" John recalls of the recording sessions, still incredulous after all these years. "Because I only had three songs written, I said, 'I'll just do old songs.' We just listened to records and said, 'Oh, let's play *this* one.' The guy who was playing drums was so shitty that I had to take his cymbals away because he'd crash them on every fucking beat."

"It was like a zoo," remembers Mike Wanchic, then on staff at Gilfoy, who would become John's regular guitarist many years later. "They asked me to sit in on the sessions. All his friends from Seymour were hanging around. The first thing I remember about John was that when I was playing on a track, he thought I wasn't playing with enough conviction, and I heard this voice come over the speaker saying, 'More *metal,* goddammit!' "

The cover songs were some of John's favorites, but the arrangements were too self-consciously "different"—all of them ill-executed, hastily recorded in one or two takes, and performed by John with a breathy, rasping, Dylan-inflected style. They included Roy Orbison's "Oh Pretty Woman," John Sebastian's "Do You Believe in Magic," Leiber and Stoller's "Jailhouse Rock" (a DeFries suggestion), and the Doors' "Twentieth Century Fox"—a bizarre lot that sounded like oddball parodies of the originals. Taking the tapes to New York, John was horrified to learn that DeFries thought they captured the essence of his sound and wanted to release them on the album, supplemented by a few of John's original compositions. John played the tapes for Mick Ronson, who asked, "What's this?" "A *record,* whaddya think!" "John," he said, "I don't know about this . . ."

"We went back into the studio and overdubbed some guitars," John says, "and Mick and I remixed it. We did it at the Hit Factory, and that's when I saw a *real* studio for the first time. I just went, 'Wow, and I've already spent my money! Can I get it back and try again?' "

While recording at the Hit Factory, John also suffered the rejection of Clive Davis, one of the recording industry's prime movers. DeFries had invited Davis down to a recording session in the hope that Clive, who had signed Bruce Springsteen to Columbia, might be interested in Mellencamp for his new label, Arista. DeFries sat with His Cliveness in the control room while, out in the studio, John did a few takes of a song called "Chestnut Street"; unfortunately, the intercom button had mistakenly been left on, which allowed John to hear Davis bluntly tell DeFries, "Nah, he doesn't have it, Tony. Not interested." That conclusion was insulting enough, but what really incensed John was Davis's courtliness when John then entered the control room afterward: "That was *wonderful!*" John almost cursed him out but he thought better of it; instead, he pretended to stumble, and in the process of losing his balance, he kicked the impeccable gentleman right in the shins. "Oh, *gee,* terribly sorry . . ."

Such displays of the old Bad Mellencamp Family Attitude only succeeded in irritating DeFries, who would hector John about how he had to grow up. John was more worried about his record. Despite his grave misgivings, DeFries seemed determined to use the cover songs on the LP. "John's fantasy was that he would come to New York," says Jamie Andrews, "and it would all happen the way it did in books. Twenty-four-track studio, only the best studio musicians—it didn't happen that way."

The original songs on the album, rehearsed and recorded with much more patience and care, are fascinating because they contain the kernel of the vision that would imbue John Mellencamp's best work in the years to come. For the most part, however, the lyrics are obviously sophomoric, like those of "American Dream":

> Well, I grew up believin' I could do what I wanted to do
> When I got a little older I found that it just wasn't true
> There's gotta be a place for me
> Where I can be just what I want to be
> Hey, but ain't that the American Dream

The song that most demonstrated at least the glimmers of songwriting promise was a ballad, "Chestnut Street Revisited," named for the main drag in Seymour that had inspired John's fantasy to be a singer in the first place. In it, he manages to cut right to the heart of his life, his town, his dreams, and the spirit of the Midwest. The song drips with frustration, insecurities, resentments—and the determination to clutch ever more tightly to the dream of success, to the belief in his destiny:

> Well, I keep hopin' and wishin' that these romantic positions
> Gonna help me hide all this pain
> And all the hurt that I felt underneath my leather-studded belt
> Of not findin' my fortune and fame
> Someday I'll blow 'em away with things that I sing and say
> I'm just a small-town boy bein' used like a toy
> And waitin' on my payday

Payday would be a long way off. Despite the promise of this ballad and his fine vocal performance on songs like "Sad Lady," written with George Green, the album was most notable for its haphazard, pedestrian qualities. The plain fact of the matter was that John Mellencamp was releasing a record years before he was prepared to, long before he even knew who he was musically. "If there's art to him at all, it's the fact that he doesn't have the slightest idea who he is and he's trying to say it in his songs," MainMan's Tony Zanetta remarked to the *Toledo Courier-Journal* in 1976. "Well, for sixteen grand, what do you expect?" John asks plaintively. "I really wish that thing never came out. The bad thing about that record is it's like having the first girl you ever made love to coming out in public to review your performance in front of the whole world, which to me would be, uh, *embarrassing*. Those old ones always come back to haunt you . . ."

In the mind of Tony DeFries, the fact that the record had been done on the cheap only meant more money to be lavished on promotion, to which he now turned his attention. First came The Look. It was decided that the cleancut appeal would be employed, and John was told, "Cut your hair." Then the record cover was shot by Jamie Andrews: "John needed that crisp, blow-dried 1970s wholesomeness," he says, "but the expression on his face was surly, the collar turned up defiantly. That was naturally *him*." Then began the search for a new name. There had been sporadic talk from the beginning of giving John a rock & roll stage name; he had indicated his willingness to consider it but had since dismissed it from his mind as something too

embarrassing to think about. "I was one of the only ones who thought there was nothing wrong with *Mellencamp,*" Andrews maintains. "After all, what kind of a name is *Springsteen?* But in Tony's mind, Mellencamp didn't fit in with the package." So, behind John's back, DeFries and Andrews and several others played around with possible monikers. Well, *Johnny* instead of John, they decided, but Johnny what?—*Puma, Mustang, Impala, Cougar*—they even tried *Johnny Indiana* before they went back to Cougar. And thus was born Johnny Cougar.

John learned of his new name when he strolled through the office one day and saw a composite of the LP cover. His breath caught in his throat, and his knees almost buckled at the sight of it: *Johnny Cougar!* What would his friends and family think? He burst into DeFries's office. "What the fuck is this Johnny Cougar shit?"

"Your new professional name," DeFries said calmly.

"What the hell's wrong with my *real* name?" John shouted apoplectically.

"I can't sell records with the name *John Mellencamp,"* said the maestro, as if addressing a particularly dense child. "I *can,* however, sell records with the name *Johnny Cougar."*

"No," John refused adamantly. "No fucking way!"

DeFries leveled his gaze at him. "Either I release a record by Johnny Cougar or there isn't going to be a record. Do you understand?"

And, so, not only did John Mellencamp sell his soul for rock & roll, but he forfeited his very name. "When I thought about it—God, what a stupid, fucking name! It was ludicrous. I didn't want to be anybody but John Mellencamp. I fought my whole life to have some kind of individuality, from grade school up. And now *Johnny Cougar* was the name that I would be known by."

Once set in motion, the wheels were impossible to stop. John had no choice but to go through with it now.

"He was talking himself into it," Cil Mellencamp relates. "The strange thing was that he'd never been known as *Johnny* his whole life by *any*body. He kept saying, 'Well, DeFries gave *Bowie* his name—and look where *he* is today,' but it bothered him." "His attitude was, 'Well, I can be Johnny Cougar and have this record deal,' " says Mark Ripley, " 'or I can be John Mellencamp and be unemployed again on Thirteenth Street.' " Given that hard choice, John acquiesced to DeFries's wishes. "He was torn, confused, but pliable—desperate to do well," says Jamie Andrews. "He did almost everything Tony said—he was smart enough to know that he had to compromise. He was desperate to be a star."

By now, the MainMan hypemobile was being greased and primed. The press began to receive releases portraying Johnny Cougar as a combination of James Dean and Bob Dylan, a kind of cartoon composite—"Bob Dean or James Dylan," as John calls it. Between the gush of the releases and the hyperbolic word of mouth, calculated to stoke expectations to preposterously high levels, several writers started phoning. "Sorry, Jawn isn't talking to the press right now." Wait a second, the reporters thought, who *is* this guy? *Mick Jagger* talks to the press! Who does he think he *is* anyway? "Jawn isn't doing any interviews until his World Debut." Well, where's that? "We'll let you know . . ."

John watched these proceedings with growing trepidation, but he could only hope—no, pray—that DeFries knew what he was doing. John certainly didn't.

When the plan was finally revealed to him, John could only roll his eyes heavenward and groan loudly. DeFries had been busy schmoozing up the town fathers of Seymour and already had the whole thing set up. What better place for little Johnny Cougar's World Debut, DeFries reasoned, than his own hometown? Each year, as is customary in many Midwestern farming communities, Seymour celebrates Oktoberfest, a sort of all-American harvest/carnival, complete with fairs and parades. By convincing him that the publicity would really put the town "on the map," DeFries had persuaded Mayor Donald H. Ernest to declare October 2, 1976, "Johnny Cougar Day" in Seymour, in recognition of the "contribution" to Oktoberfest made by Johnny Cougar "as a member of the community with special and unique talents as an entertainer and performer"—so reads the official proclamation. There would be a parade right down Chestnut, complete with limousines, capped off by a concert; the world premiere of the nation's newest rock sensation at—where else?—the Seymour Armory at Freeman Field. Main-Man was planning on airlifting in a corps of the rock press to cover the event. "No, not that!" John pleaded helplessly. *"Please,* anything but that!"

"He was mortified, to say the least," offers Jamie Andrews, still chuckling at John's reaction. "His fantasy had been to get *out* of there and to be a star in New York, and here we were bringing him right back to the very people he wanted to get away from! He was petrified nobody would come to the show at the Armory because he couldn't get people to come see him in the lounges. But we were determined to fill that Armory. . . . We figured he was the first person in Seymour who ever got a shot at being famous and that this would be the most exciting thing that happened in the town since a tornado came and blew the mayor's house away. Carter was running for the presidency at the time, so we tried to get him; then we tried the governor, Miss Lillian—he was nervous, poor baby." Did MainMan exhibit any concern whatever for John's feelings at the time? "Oh, we felt bad that he was so embarrassed," says Jamie. "But he knew that he was risking total humiliation by coming to MainMan. He was embarrassed by everything we did."

There wasn't even enough time for a nervous breakdown. Determined not to make a fool of himself at the concert, John assembled a band and started rehearsing in a small theater in Brownstown. The group comprised Larry Crane on guitar, Dave Parman on bass, Wayne Idall on sax, Terry Sala on drums, and Bub Wince on piano; rehearsals were going well until some townspeople complained that a bunch of "degenerates" were making a ruckus. The Tiger Force Band was summarily run out of town.

Back in Seymour, preparations went ahead, and people were agog at the hoopla. Marilyn Mellencamp was enjoying the attention. "If you took it all in

Larry Crane, John and Cil, flanked by the Cougarettes, Johnny Cougar Day, October 2, 1976.

stride, it was *fun*," she says. "DeFries came in and went down to the bank and plopped down $100,000 on deposit. When you do that in Seymour, you get people's attention." "It was the biggest hype I've ever seen," says Ted Mellencamp. "Of course, at the time, if DeFries had told us to go shit in buckets, we would have done it."

John's friends were bowled over by the whole plan—they stood around amazed, laughing at him. George Green recalls, "I loved the irony of it. First the people of Seymour wouldn't give him the *time* of day. Now they were giving him his *own* day!" Some people who had previously hated John were suddenly displaying an obsequiousness toward him that he found nauseating; others were openly contemptuous. "A lot of people sour-graped him because they were jealous," says Dave Knotts. "They were wishing it was them instead of him." Most people, however, were simply incredulous: "The general attitude around town was, 'Ah, shit, Mellencamp's got some guy with more money than sense behind him who thinks he's gonna make him a *star*,' " Tim Elsner points out. "They were more embarrassed for him than anything else . . ."

John tried to take it all in stride. "He tried being very matter-of-fact about it all," relates Gary Boebinger. "He'd tell me about the limos and the Lear jets and everything, but with a tone of voice like, 'Now, Bo, I know you're not gonna *believe* this, but this shit is *normal* for this business!' " Of course, it wasn't easy staying calm when you'd come home to find out that your five-year-old's teacher had called ("Isn't your last name Mellencamp? Michelle insists it's Cougar!") and wants you to come in for show-and-tell; or that a National Johnny Cougar Fan Club had just been formed, with your sister as president.

Johnny Cougar Day dawned bright and clear over southern Indiana. It was one of those classic Midwestern fall days, with an Indian summer sun sparkling through the brilliant autumnal foliage, toasting the treelined streets. At midday, the sound of whistles was heard in downtown Seymour as the parade began. In perfect formation, with drum majorettes kicking high, the Seymour High marching band led the procession, followed by a bunch of kids coaching a pack of dogs through what talk show host David Letterman now calls "stupid pet tricks." Then came two long Cadillac limos led by a bright blue sports car, surrounded by a group of teenage girls with yellow T-shirts that read *Johnny Cougar* (the Cougarettes) as a PA announced, "MCA recording artist Johnny Cougar!"—and the kids screamed and clapped as if the Beatles were coming.

The hero himself protruded through the sun roof of the first limo, with Cil at his side, waving in a perfunctory manner, with an expression on his face as if he were suffering from a very severe case of prickly heat on his rear end, exacerbated by a too-tight pair of underpants. Passing people with puzzled looks who were seated in lawn chairs in their front yards, he kept hearing, "What's a Johnny Kreuger?" Occasionally, he perked up enough to wave to somebody he knew or to smile at a girl, but then his expression would change when he passed a group of kids who flipped him the bird and shouted, "Hey, Mellencamp, you *asshole*!" He was followed by the Jackson County Pork Queen and by the Ambitious Young Farmers Float.

With his penchant for theatrical overkill, Tony DeFries had wanted Johnny Cougar to be lowered by helicopter onto the site of his debut concert, waving to the throngs from a rope ladder like some rock & roll daredevil or swashbuckler. The plan fell through, however, and DeFries had to be content with a huge pair of searchlights crisscrossing beams through the night sky above Freeman Field, lending the scene the aura of a Hollywood premiere as thousands of people filed into the Armory, a cavernous structure that resembled an airplane hangar. The front rows of the folding chairs were filled with every Mellencamp in the phone book, all of them with eyes riveted on the stage, by MCA representatives, and by writers and editors from *Rolling Stone, Creem,* the *Village Voice, Penthouse,* the *Daily News,* the *Boston*

World Debut concert at the Freeman Field Armory.

Globe—just about every publication that MainMan could sweet-talk into jumping on a free junket to the middle of Indiana. The pressure was bad enough, but death threats had been phoned in before the performance ("It was probably some kid I beat up in junior high school trying to get back at me," John says), and the star had to worry about somebody taking a shot at him. "That was the most scared I've ever been in my life," Larry Crane recalls. "There were two thousand people out there—*every*body we ever knew in our lives! Right before we went onstage, I puked my guts out."

The lights went out, a roar went up, and a neon sign that read *Johnny Cougar: Chestnut Street Revisited* began flashing to the left of the stage; the spotlight then picked up a fifteen-year-old girl named Lea at centerstage with a harp, who began to pluck the bathetic strains of "Somewhere over the Rainbow." And then pandemonium erupted as Johnny Cougar himself appeared, alone, with an acoustic guitar—a rather courageous homage to Dylan—to sing "Chestnut Street." "Hello, I'm Johnny Cougar, and this is Tiger Force!" The tightly rehearsed band broke out into a muscular, blazing rock instrumental amid a well-designed light show, and John was off and running. Midway through the performance he stripped off his tight black T-shirt. "Boy, he was a nervous sonofabitch up there," Mark Ripley says. "He had this habit when he was nervous in those days—he'd stagger. He really didn't have an act down or anything—it was all raw energy—and the more nervous he got, the more he'd stagger. It looked like he was punchdrunk up there." "Whenever it came time for him to talk," recalls Cil Mellencamp, "you just knew *fuck* was going to be the first word out of his mouth. It was a nervous reaction, but a lot of people were scandalized." Every time he felt a lull in the performance, he drove himself and the band to full tilt, pushing his whole being angrily, violently higher. By the final song he was prancing, grabbing the bouquets at the lap of the stage, and flinging the flowers into the dancing and screaming audience. The band walked off, and suddenly the place was filled with a sea of lighted matches—this was the real thing! John walked back out panting, drenched in sweat, and sang the Stones' "Brown Sugar" for his encore. He returned to centerstage to accept some bouquets from a prom queen and flung them right back into the audience. For a moment he just stood there, a look of triumphant astonishment on his face, walked off, and promptly collapsed backstage from nervous exhaustion. It was the beginning of a performing style that would carry him through the years—a style characterized by profanity; the willingness to subsist on nothing more than naked, nervous energy; and the ethos of the party—of having a good time— exalted above all else.

"The concert itself was as great as you'd expect from a punk who gets to come back and take revenge on his own high school," wrote Rick Johnson in *The Beat Goes On*. "Wouldn't *you* love to do that?"

The publicity campaign kicked off inauspiciously when the press arrived for the party at Richard and Marilyn's at the exact moment that Janet Mellencamp was having a knock-down, drag-out fight with her boyfriend. "She was so mad at him that she took a cane and broke it across his back," relates Marilyn. "We thought it was funny, of course—but some of them were aghast."

The journalists who'd flown in for Johnny Cougar's world debut were all booked into the Seymour Holiday Inn. During their several days in town, they were given "access" to the new star for his first interviews. Most of them had already listened to—and disliked—the album; they'd come along either to enjoy the free press junket or because they sensed an amusing story in the offing. Given their biased attitudes and Johnny Cougar's unguarded garrulousness ("I could never really believe anybody would want to interview me in the first place!"), not to mention the controversial and commanding Tony De-

Fries, the first images of Cougar to emerge in the press were very erratic. Because Cougar was a total unknown, MainMan operated under the assumption that *any* publicity was better than no publicity at all; they had at least succeeded in ensuring him a few well-placed stories. What emerged, however, was potentially disastrous for his nascent career—the image of an arrogant, overconfident kid shooting his mouth off about everything.

"Everybody in the press kept wondering what the connection was between Cougar and Bowie, and it was so bizarre because of the contrast," recalls Martin Cerf, then at *Phonograph Records*. "It piqued people's interest and made John newsworthy, even if they didn't like the record. In spite of the bad taste and the poor packaging, it was obvious there was something interesting there. The rejection only made him more determined to persevere, and for an artist coming from nowhere he had a spontaneous kind of confidence that someone at his stage rarely possesses."

"I just have a feeling that I'm going to be a success," Johnny Cougar told

(J. I. C. Andrews/MainMan)

Zach Dunkin of the *Indianapolis Times,* in a November 1, 1976, story headlined JOHNNY COUGAR CONFIDENT. "I always knew at least this much would happen, and now I know that the rest is going to happen, too." He "looks like Peter Pan turned uptown hustler," wrote Stephen Gaines in a profile titled "A Star Blooms amid the Indiana Corn" in the New York *Daily News*. "He's just as infatuated with himself as Muhammad Ali." Despite John's brash cockiness, most of the writers who actually spent time with him ended up liking him. "I walked away convinced that he would, in fact, become a star," ventured Bob Sloane in the *Primo Times*. "I further found that I liked him as a person. He is highly emotional, sensitive, and intelligent, but blessed/cursed with a vision that sees the utter bullshit in everything."

In the first series of pieces about him, John's penchant for saying what was on his mind, in no uncertain terms, took the form of broadsides against church, home, society, small towns, and the critics who were quick to suggest that his dream was being packaged and sold like soapsuds. In his bravado emerged the posture of the Angry Young Man, a stance as old as rock & roll itself. "What has this country come to after all?" he responded to the *Toledo Courier-Journal*. "I'll tell you. It's nothing but strips and trash, hamburger joints, and the same old tired faces going nowhere. They've taken all the fun out of life. That's why people take themselves so seriously, because they've got nothing else to do but think about themselves. Just look around you, man. There's a hell of a lot more second- and third-rate cities in the United States than first-class cities. And the fact is, you can sell telephone books to the American public if you package and advertise them."

Obviously, John had no conceivable idea of how his statements could be taken and used out of context by a press that was waiting to throw him to the lions. He just blithely blundered on, dutifully filling their notebooks and tape recorders with his impressions. Moreover, DeFries himself tried to stir up publicity with his own inflammatory comments, the most controversial of which concerned his ex-client, David Bowie. DeFries told the *Technician* of Raleigh, North Carolina: "Johnny really hates everything Bowie is for. He once told me, 'Anyone who can get headlines for an orange-haired, no-talent, limey faggot like David Bowie can do anything.'" Naturally, the statement stuck in the throat of the press like a chicken bone, gagging them; and John was mortified. "I *never* said that!" he maintains. "Why would I ever say that? The only reason I was at MainMan in the first place was because I was such a big Bowie fan . . ."

Such was the atmosphere surrounding Johnny Cougar as he undertook his very first tour, from October 2 to 16, 1976, playing five dates in Indiana—

Columbus, Franklin, Terre Haute, Huntington, Madison—and then the Memorial Auditorium in Louisville, Kentucky. "We couldn't fill the theaters," says Jamie Andrews, "so we hired a bus and brought in the Cougarettes from Seymour with their parents." "It was on the job training," John says. "There I was with my three songs—and I'd only been onstage about ten times in my life—on tour, right?" "Nobody had *any* idea of what was going on," adds Ted Mellencamp, who was hired on the tour as a roadie. "We began to see how valuable it was to be able to throw money around. At the Crump Theater in Columbus, we wanted to move the great big movie screen for the show, and they said no; I started waving hundred dollar bills and, boy, they moved it pretty fast."

With tickets priced at $5, the tour was a commercial failure, although it had its benefits. Zach Dunkin saw both the opening of the tour in Seymour and the final show in Louisville. "One could see Cougar and his Tiger Force had gained valuable confidence and poise over the month," he noted in the *Indianapolis Times*.

While more dates were scheduled, MainMan tried to galvanize MCA into promoting *Chestnut Street Incident,* but the record was sinking without a trace. Reviews were almost nonexistent, and those who actually *did* write about *Chestnut Street* did so with the kind of gleeful derision reserved for the most memorable Broadway flops ("What a divine find this album will be in the bargain bins of 1984!" predicted Richard Riegal of *Creem*.)

Ironically, the greatest resistance to the record came not from the press, but from John's own record company, which now steadfastly refused to get behind it, although Jon Scott and Dave Loncao, two young MCA promotion men, immediately recognized Cougar's promise. MCA had sent Scott to Seymour to scout Cougar's debut at the Armory. "They wanted to know if he was any damn good because nobody had ever seen him live," Scott says, "and I sat there in the front row and he just blew me away. I went back to the company and it took a lot of coercing to even get a little money for promotion."

MCA disliked Cougar's rebel image, but they apparently disliked his manager even more. "DeFries was very demanding," Scott continues. "He wanted some big neon billboard in Hollywood and the shit really hit the fan over that." Scott only managed to weasel enough money out of MCA for one local promotion in Los Angeles. "We took a live cougar to the Tower Records parking lot and to all the radio stations in the city—that was my idea. The cat started getting testy after a while and somebody almost got killed! It cost over a thousand dollars, and everybody thought I was crazy."

Nevertheless, Scott refused to give in and to let the album die. "I used to haunt J. J. Jackson in Los Angeles, trying to get him to play the record on his station. Once I found him sleeping on a plane and stuck a cassette in his ear—it never worked. Then I took it to WMMS in Cleveland, and we finally broke through there because DeFries was John's manager and Cleveland was a big Bowie town."

The first and one of the only disk jockeys to play Johnny Cougar in the United States was Kid Leo, on WMMS's afternoon show. "The cover songs like 'Oh Pretty Woman' were terrible," Leo recalls, "but on 'Chestnut Street,' you could see the raw talent as a singer/songwriter. I'm a lyrics man and a big fan of Bruce Springsteen, and what I saw in Cougar was essentially an urban look at things, but from a small town point of view. I believed he was really going someplace and we played the record some—but the reaction was only minimal."

The beachhead at WMMS, an extremely important market for any new artist, had been made only after the incredible persistence of Dave Loncao, the other young promo man at MCA who believed in Cougar and found himself frustrated at every turn. "I organized a concert for him at the University of Toledo," Loncao says, "because the local station there had been one of the few that had responded to his music. I remember how serious John was about that show—and, for one reason or another, he bombed. There were thousands of people, and by the end of the show there were maybe one-third of them left. I could identify with him, though. It was easy to recognize the three most important things in his life: Marlboros, Coca-Cola, and his favorite, most expressive word—*fuck*. He used any one of the three at least every thirty seconds. He was interviewed at the station, and I remember him cursing on the air and the program director looking at me like, 'What the hell is *this*?' "

It was clear to MainMan that Johnny Cougar's album was stiffing, despite all the hype and gimmicks. "We had a car going from one end of the country to the other," says Jamie Andrews, "and we had somebody in it buying a record in every town, wherever they could find it—just so there'd be *some* demand." The strategy didn't work and *Chestnut Street Incident,* which sold approximately twelve thousand units—mostly in Indiana—was soon history. When John received his very first royalty check, dated December 16, 1977, the amount was $27.59.

Well, not to worry, John told himself—just don't blow the second album! He fully admitted to himself how embarrassingly bad the first effort had been, compared to what he now felt capable of producing. The second record is critical in the progressive development of an artist: It must serve notice to record company, to critical establishment, and to the public that the artist has grown—that the promise presumably displayed by the debut effort has been consolidated. Naturally, as the record company invests more money, the pressure rises for a song on the charts and for good reviews. Considering his misbegotten first effort, what Johnny Cougar faced was a comprehensive need to redeem himself and to wipe the egg from his face. He set about his second record determined to write and produce everything himself. The first record had cost $16,000; now he would spend $65,000 on the second. Instead of some dipshit studio in Bloomington, he would record at the Hit Factory in New York. He'd show the sonsofbitches . . .

"You could say I was coming down to earth pretty hard," John says. "In the beginning, I guess I started believing the hype myself to a degree—it happened to Bowie, too, because DeFries would tell you you're the greatest thing in the world and there you are at twenty-four staying in the biggest hotel, being driven around in some limousine. After the illusion wore off in about six months, I realized you really had to get out there and work hard at it."

"Unlike the first record, we did a lot of rehearsing and arranging this time," Larry Crane comments. "The songs were musically a lot more interesting, more rock-oriented. That's when I started realizing that John could be a really good songwriter one day. We knew what we wanted to do—the problem was that we didn't know *how* to do it."

The theme of the second record, for the most part, derived from what had happened to John since he'd set out to fulfill his dream. The music was more controlled, sophisticated, energetic; the lyrics, more cynical and consciously tongue-in-cheek; and the band was certainly tighter, more polished after the experience of their first couple of tours. However, it was the studio this time, with its mystifying technology, that proved their undoing: The production is muddled, poorly mixed—sometimes whole phrases of lyrics are garbled and lost. Even so, *The Kid Inside* did represent a significant leap forward. The title track begins with sweet acoustic guitars and gets successively nastier, more raucous with each verse.

> I press my face against the window
> I run my fingers through my hair
> I watch my life go round in circles
> And I realize that nobody but me cares.

The voice is that of a perennial outsider, someone who has been roughed up, injured: "It's so easy to see that my wounds have been opened wide," he sings on the refrain. "And you can just kid the Kid inside so many times."

This theme is also explored in an evocative ballad called "Sidewalks and Streetlights":

> Gonna make me a big star
> Or haven't you heard yet
> Don't know how it's going to go
> I'm too young to know
> And if it's just my name, well, hell,
> I can change it . . .

John sings the song with raw emotion, his phrasing fluctuating from brilliant to sloppy; the verses are haunted by the guitar of Larry Crane and the sax of Wayne Hall, giving the song the air of a cheap cabaret. "Too Young to Live" is an anthem to teenage angst; "American Son," with its slashing wall of sound guitar chords, is a homage to Bowie's "Suffragette City"; "Gearhead," a ballad with twelve-string guitar, sounds like vintage Jefferson Airplane, circa 1967.

While the album was being recorded at the Hit Factory in New York, John and the band were ensconced at the St. Moritz, living like little kings. "All our expenses were taken care of," recalls Larry Crane, "and we were soakin' in the cash, making about three hundred a week and spending it as quick as we could get it. We'd wander the streets and hang out at places like One Fifth Avenue and Ashleigh's, which was the hot club for the music people at the time. We also got to take in a bit more of the New York music scene, which was fun for us—go over to CBGB's and see Patti Smith or the Talking Heads. It was a great time . . ."

John's idea of a good time was to ferry in friends and family from Indiana and unleash them in New York. Of course, one of the first victims was Mark Ripley. "One night after a mixing session, Jamie had us limoed over to Ashleigh's," Ripley recalls. "It was me, Parman, and John—just hicks loose in the big city. Jamie was ordering liver paté and expensive wine, and we all got drunk—except John, of course—and went upstairs to the disco and went hog-wild. Of course, the limo driver was the only one who scored. Later, when we stumbled out of the place, we opened the back door of the car, and there he was screwing some girl in the backseat. I remember thinking, So *this* is the music business!''

The next person to be imported was Speck Mellencamp. "Grandpa had never been on a plane, never been out of Indiana," Ripley says, "so John said, 'Fuck, we'll kill two birds with one stone!' It was wild. John picked him up at the airport and limoed him to the St. Moritz. 'Now, Grandpa, what do you think about all this! Look at us driving around here in a big fucking limousine!' He was laughing his head off. Grandpa kept saying, 'I'm with ya, boy!' ''

Tony DeFries watched these goings-on with detached amusement. He tolerated John's antics with the understanding that his word was law. "We were all afraid of him," John says. "We felt that it was by the grace of God that he was allowing us to make records. But we made fun of him, too. We called him Fuzz-wuzz and Kinky Big Nose behind his back."

As the record neared completion, John became increasingly argumentative and difficult about the promotional schemes. For one thing, he was terrified about the new look that Jamie Andrews wanted to give him for the album cover. "He was heading more toward rock in his music," Jamie says. "The all-American image didn't work, so we thought we'd turn him into a pretty boy and give him the look of one of those sexy French magazine covers. That's when he became resistant and started to freak."

The photo session took place in the bathroom of what had been Marilyn Monroe and Joe DiMaggio's honeymoon suite at the Lexington Hotel. Clad in a blue terrycloth bathrobe, with a red towel around his neck, with his now-long hair wetted down and a heavy sheen of makeup and lip gloss applied by Suzy Ronson, Johnny Cougar was transformed from an all-American hustler into an androgynous version of David Cassidy. "Those are the photos he really loves to hate," Jamie recognizes. "He was appalled when he saw them!" As it turned out, John's apprehensions about the image were well founded. When MainMan eventually released the record some six years later, the photo of John used for the cover, with his hands clasped behind his head and his lips parted in supplication, made him look like a schoolboy who had been beaten and sodomized and forced to pose against his will for the cover of some perverted magazine.

As it came time to deliver the record to MCA, tension mounted. "One morning I woke up in the St. Moritz," remembers John, "and there was Dave Parman, crying, really upset. I said, 'What the hell's the matter?' And he says, 'I can't take all this pressure!' I didn't know what he was talking about: 'What pressure?' 'We're gonna be big stars,' he says, 'and I don't know if I

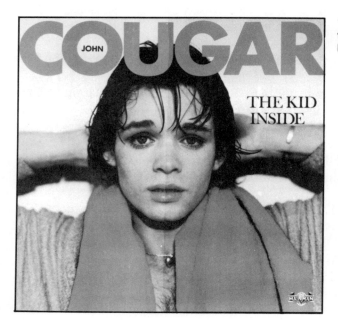

can handle it!' I couldn't believe it . . . 'Yeah, but we're not *stars,'* I told him. 'We're nobody, we're just a bunch of kids riding around in limousines!' ''

On the very day that MainMan delivered *The Kid Inside,* a massive corporate shakeup convulsed MCA, sweeping away every one of its top executives from Mike Maitland on down, leaving only Vince Cosgrove, the radio promo man who had detested Johnny Cougar the most. In fact, within the new power structure, the signing of Johnny Cougar was being held up as a prime example of the mistakes of the old guard—glaring evidence of bad judgment. All John's supporters within the company—Bob Davis, Jon Scott, Dave Loncao—were subsequently fired; the company paid MainMan for the record and refused to release it.

John was crushed. Six months went by without MainMan being able to get a deal going. "Nobody would touch him," Jamie Andrews recalls, "and Tony got disillusioned. He's like the stock market—up and down."

"Well," DeFries told John. "I think it's time to call it quits."

"Right," responded John, crestfallen. What else was there to say?

The split with MainMan was an easy one compared to what had transpired between DeFries and artists like Bowie and Iggy—of course, it might have been very different had John been making a lot of money. According to Jamie Andrews, "It was Tony's policy to always take a part of the future. Each time an artist split, we had a different deal; with David, we had percentages. I told

Tony to let John go free, and Tony agreed because he knew how difficult it would have been for him to find another manager with that override hanging over him. We did make our money back from MCA on what we'd spent on the record, but we still were owed money on what we'd spent on *him,* so we made a deal that as soon as we recouped our costs with the two records, we'd split all profits after that." "It wasn't like DeFries was doing me a favor," John elaborates. "It was easier that way. He was as fed up with me as I was with him, and he just wanted to get rid of me. It's true that he might not have wanted to saddle me, but he didn't really think I was going to amount to anything at that point anyway."

It all seemed to end as quickly, as unexpectedly as it had started—with John Mellencamp stunned. The bottom line was that, in the business, Johnny Cougar was a bad joke. People knew him by his first record, an unmitigated disaster, and by a name that he hated. "When I left MainMan," he says, "I'd try to call people and say, 'This is John Mellencamp,' and they'd hang up. I was stuck with Cougar." His second record, he realized, might never see the light of day, and even if it did, he would have absolutely no control over it. Heartbroken, he limped back home to Indiana with a reputation for "bad attitude" that would have sobered Sid Vicious. "I didn't know what to do," he says. "I felt like it was fourth down, long yardage. Time to drop back and punt . . ."

Back in Indiana, the implications of the MainMan debacle began to hit home. "John was really upset," confides Cil, "because he at least had been happier with that second album—he really wanted it to come out. He was shaken up, but he was determined to go on and try and get something else together. The problem was I didn't know how long it would take or how we'd survive . . ."

The first thing he decided to do was to get out of Seymour. It was very distressing to be living back in his home town, the site of Johnny Cougar Day and other such abominations. His local notoriety definitely had its disadvantages. "I left for a week and someone broke into my house," reveals John. "I came back and somebody had been using my bed! They just broke in because it was *my* house; they wanted to be able to say, 'I made it in Johnny Cougar's bed.' I just left." They moved into a modest apartment complex in Bloomington; Cil wasted no time getting a job in a local department store.

The first thing that happened was the disbanding of Tiger Force. "John said, 'Look you guys, the well has run dry,' " says Larry Crane. " 'You go ahead and do what you have to do and I'll see what I can come up with.' " Several guys in the band, particularly Dave Parman, were bitter. "Everybody thought

I had blown it," John says. "Their attitude was, 'It's all over. You get one big chance in life and you fucked it up.' " Of the old band, John realized that the only one he could count on, the one who still had faith in him, was Larry Crane. "Most people don't know what they want, but John always has an idea," Crane observes."He didn't know exactly, but at least he pointed himself in the right direction."

The right direction this time was Los Angeles. Bob Davis, who'd been Mike Maitland's henchman at MCA, was offering to shop John to another manager. An established player well versed in both the legal and A&R sides of the business, Davis had been the force behind Johnny Cougar's original signing. John didn't completely trust him—with his long hair, the gold chains around his neck, and his aviator's sunglasses, Davis seemed the epitome of the terminally cool, high-living, Hollywood music-business type—but at least he was a sincere fan. So, John packed things and headed out there, staying with Davis for six weeks while phone calls were made. "The only thing I told him was, no flakes this time," John says. "I've already had one flake manager and that's enough."

Acting as John's personal attorney, Davis talked to four managers who displayed varying levels of interest, until John met Billy Gaff, the flamboyant British manager of superstar Rod Stewart. Another high-powered, high-

"Isn't you're name Mellencamp? Michelle keeps insisting its *Cougar . . .*"

profile independent power broker in the industry, Gaff devoted himself to Stewart almost exclusively, who was at the zenith of his career. When Gaff expressed interest in seeing him, John wasted no time heading over to the huge Spanish-style home in Beverly Hills, bringing his acoustic guitar. "I thought these manager types had information that was somehow illegal for a dumb kid from Indiana to possess," John reflects. "After all, who was I? These guys did business with Elton John and Rod Stewart!"

Walking into the pool area, John encountered a suntanned, bare-chested man pruning hedges and trees, sweating in the sun. "I thought it was some gardener, but it was really Gaff, throwing a fit," John laughs. "He was mad at the people who'd been staying at his house for not taking care of the grounds, so he was doing it himself." They sat down and talked for five hours, and John took out his guitar and played him a recently penned ballad called "Taxi Dancer," about a girl from California with a dream.

> Well she started out to be a dancer
> She's gonna make her livin' dancin' in
>   the Broadway shows
> So she hitchhiked cross country from
>   Pasaroba to the Big Red Apple
> Where your dreams are made, and your
>   debts must be paid on time.

A shrewd businessman, Gaff recognized that John needed time and space to consolidate his talent. He liked the song but at first was noncommittal about offering John a deal. Still, John recalls, "He said he'd support me all summer while I put a new band together and wrote new material. Then, in about four to five months, he'd come out to look at what I'd done. If he liked it, he said we'd make a deal." John felt immediately comfortable with the arrangement. "What I liked about him was that it seemed he had no need to get his hands on me," he says. "He'd already been so successful with Rod Stewart that I felt he wouldn't have the need to try to make me into something that I wasn't."

With $1,200 a month from Gaff, John rented a big, rambling old house out in Ellotsville for his band and started scrounging about for new musicians. "I was making seventeen dollars a week, living in the back of some old lady's house," Larry Crane remembers. "John had heard about this music store in St. Louis from Mick Ronson where you could get hooked up with musicians, and that's how we found Tom Knowles, the drummer, and Robert Frank, or

'Ferd' as we called him, on bass. We auditioned them at Mark Ripley's house in Seymour.'' Ferd and Knowles soon moved to Bloomington; John called the new group *Streethart*.

John now turned his attention to songwriting. The first thing he decided was that he'd had enough of purely autobiographical songs for a while. He got an inspiration for one good song from his old buddy, Jay Nicholson, who had fallen on hard times with drugs and alcohol since his days as Seymour High's heartthrob. John went to visit him one day at his house, hoping to rouse Jay from his deep funk. "He was all fucked up," John recounts, "and he told me he was going to kill himself. I said, 'Hey, what's your *problem?*' And he said, 'Man, I need to find some chick I can be with who won't bug the shit out of me.' '' The sentiment reminded him of the line from a Stones' song: "I need a lover who'll make me happy . . .'' The theme seemed obvious and accessible enough. He started with the chorus:

> I need a lover that won't drive me crazy
> Some girl to thrill me and then go away
> I need a lover that won't drive me crazy
> Some girl that knows the meaning of
> Hey, hit the highway.

The verses came easily—he simply envisioned Nicholson's lonely, frustrated existence: "Well, I'm not asking to be loved or forgiven/I just can't face shakin' in this bedroom one more night alone.'' As he worked on it, the band members found the words too churlish, yet it was undeniably honest: He had expressed nothing more than the most visceral male desire for the thrill of sex without the emotional commitment of intimacy. John wanted the song to be a hard rocker, heaving with guitars and driven along by machine gun–like drumming—a song that he could shout hoarsely, violently, but not before a long, teasing introduction with intricate chord changes, mounted to a shattering crescendo. Of course, as the band went about working out the number, roughing up different versions, it never occurred to any of them that John had written a song that would come to epitomize the sexual ambience of the 1970s.

John and Streethart had the opportunity to try out the new song when they booked what they thought would be a showcase appearance at Beginnings, a club in the Italian section of Chicago. Gaff decided to send his lieutenant, Mike Gill, to scout the gig and to report his impressions. The band loaded their equipment in an old van and headed for the Second City. "It was Halloween night,'' recalls Ted Mellencamp, "and we got every crazy we could to follow us up there and pack the place to make it seem like John had a big following." "We thought it was going to be a regular gig," Crane elaborates, "and it turned out to be a talent night! We were freaked—there were all these bands waiting to audition. So Mike Gill and Bob Davis come driving up in this limo, and we played the show as if it were the Fillmore or something." Gill, who had developed such bands as Atomic Rooster in England, was impressed.

Not too long after this encounter, Gaff set up an appearance for John at the Whiskey A Go-Go in Los Angeles. John and his band were slated to open for the Jam, a British punk band making their first U.S. appearance, who were supposed to be the Next Big Thing. The plan had been to reintroduce John to the American music scene following the MainMan catastrophe, but it turned out to be a classic manifestation of the Bad Mellencamp Family Attitude. "We all came out in army fatigues," John recalls. "I was into this really stupid thing about how the rock and roll business was like being in a war. I made a lot of enemies that night because I was so obnoxious. When I think people won't like me, my first defense is to not like them first. The first words out of my mouth were, 'Fuck you, I *hate* you . . .' "

Cougar was right about one thing: The punked-out kids, many with their heads gaffer-taped (the latest craze), did *not* like him. "The audience were fanatic anglophiles—all these nouveau riche Beverly Hills punks who'd come to see the Jam," recalls Polygram A&R man Jerry Jaffee, also in attendance that night, "and here were these kids from Indiana dressed as soldiers! It was amazing John even survived it—they wanted him off that stage pretty badly. He opened with "I Need a Lover," and I said to myself, "Hit song!" I looked over at Mike Chapman, who was taking notes furiously . . ."

Producer Mike Chapman, who'd worked with Blondie and was about to produce Suzy Quatro, wasted no time finding his way backstage after the show. There he encountered a despondent John Cougar and begged him to allow Quatro to do the song. "Yeah, sure, why not," said John, flattered, thinking that maybe the evening wasn't such a disaster after all. He thought very little about Chapman's request at the time, but soon had a startling bit of news for his band. "Boys, pack your bags—we're going to England to make a record!"

Gaff's plan was based on one hard, simple fact: Still no American record company wanted any part of Johnny Cougar. By importing Johnny and Streethart to London, they could at least cut a record on Riva, Gaff's independent label, which did not as yet have distribution set up in the United

States. John was under the assumption that he'd only be staying long enough to record an album—several months at most. They arrived in November 1977, and Gaff set them all up in a townhouse on the King's Road. John signed his deal with Riva once again without benefit of attorney. Cil had Michelle enrolled in London's American School and took over the running of the house. "It was just me and the band," she says. "I did all the shopping, the cleaning. I loved it over there." John felt differently. "For me, it was more like culture shock. At Thanksgiving, the turkey cost about forty dollars and it still had the feathers on it! I said, 'What the hell's *this?'* "

An interesting producer was engaged for the LP: John Punter, the innovative alumnus of Roxy Music. Even though Punter approached John with an open mind and a smile on his face, the experience of making *A Biography* was not a happy one. "I had a big chip on my shoulder during that album," John recognizes. "It was too soon after the MainMan thing, and I was still pissed off about it. You know, I just felt like a fucking fool after that. My life in general was fucked up and so was my attitude. It was just one of those bad periods you go through when you hate everything . . . It lasted about two years."

The record, which cost $43,000 to make, would never be released in the United States, and yet it would prove crucial to John's career. Tracks were laid down at Wessex Studio in December, overdubs were done at Basing Street, and vocals and mixing at George Martin's Air Studios through February. The music was tougher and much more accomplished; the lyrics were solemn, angry, very downbeat. Punter's production was quirky and playful but always controlled. The truly notable developments were the breakthrough of Larry Crane's musicianship, John's growing confidence as a vocalist, and a song that classifies as a minor rock masterpiece—"I Need a Lover."

John had kept the song in the back of his mind, and Punter's reaction to it had been immediate: It had the hook of a potential hit, it got the blood going, but it was different. Punter's contribution was to maximize the musical conflicts of the song, contrasting the impeccable clarity of the sound with the raw, untamed quality of the vocals. Larry Crane's addition was his brilliantly arranged introduction. "I was really into trying to stack the sound of the guitars," Crane says. "I wanted to get an orchestrated rock and roll feeling. We spent hours and hours in the studio; I sat down and mathematically figured out all the chord changes. Every twelve bars it changes keys."

The photo that became the cover of *A Biography* also lined the tubes of London by the thousands.

The album contained other surprises. "Taxi Dancer," the ballad that John had played for Gaff in Los Angeles, had developed into his finest piece of pure songwriting so far. John turned the Broadway dream of the dancer into a poignant portrait of lost innocence and shattered dreams; the girl takes a job cleaning up at the Gramercy Park Hotel, then supplements her income by getting a job "dancing in a bar"—presumably a sleazy ballroom. In the end, we see her broken, drunk in a bar on Forty-second Street. Yet the person telling her story so understands her pain that he's determined to love her, dance with her, soothe her—even if it means getting lost in the same hopeless illusions. "Night Slumming," which opens with two acoustic blues guitars, one picking notes and the other a twanging slide, bursts into the most serious rock song of John's career—a harbinger of things to come. "Let Them Run Your Life," on the other hand, is the most concise expression so far of what was becoming John's obsessional theme—rebellion. The song is served up almost as an old-fashioned, protest-style folk song, with Dylanesque overtones:

> Hello girls and boys
> As you sit in your carpeted bedrooms with your stereos on
> Playin' with those hundred-dollar toys
> Built to occupy your minds so you don't know your futures are gone

Filled with rage at a system where people have to "kiss the ass of the authorities" to survive, he delivers the song in a righteous admonitory tone that would turn many critics off: "And me I'm so misunderstood but I'm still alive," it concludes, "My eyes are open wide to the fact that the world just might lie." The bitter, uncompromising words reflect the fact that the songwriter was passing through one of the most cynical periods of his life.

Clearly, he was not about to go as naïvely down the primrose paths of packaging and hype again without kicking and screaming. When Gaff decided on a high-profile promotion campaign to try to sell Johnny Cougar to the British, John told him, "Listen, I don't know if I want this shit done—I've had this done before."

"But not by me," was Gaff's retort.

Sounds magazine reported that Gaff had invested £150,000 in a promotional campaign for Johnny Cougar, which included glossy bios, full-page ads, and— what really mortified John—posters in the tubes of London. The poster was a reproduction of the image that would be used for the LP cover, a photo by David Steen of John in an old double-breasted sports jacket, hands in pockets,

but done in a rich sepia tint. "It was a really pretty picture," Larry Crane says, "and John despised it. It looked like an ad for a cologne or something! One day we went down into the tubes and there were literally *thousands* of them—you couldn't go anywhere in London without seeing it. At the time, our feeling was that hype was exactly what we didn't need—we needed to establish ourselves as artists. One look at those pictures and we knew we were gonna have credibility problems. John was so angry that he'd just rip them off the walls! You'd see him walking along the platform furiously tearing down these images of himself . . ."

Johnny Cougar's credibility problems weren't helped by making certain promotional appearances at Gaff's behest in pop magazines catering to teenyboppers. That year, he found himself on the cover of *My Guy* ("True Life, True Love—In Photo Stories!"), as *Pink* "Superstar," and in June as *Oh Boy!* "Hunk of the Month." Looking back at those experiences, John moans, "God, how humiliating . . ."

"Billy Gaff probably felt it was the same approach he'd taken with Rod Stewart," comments Martin Cerf, who would soon go to work for the Riva organization. "It obviously wasn't what John wanted. As bad as the reception to the first Johnny Cougar LP had been in America, it was ten times worse in England. It went totally against the grain of what was happening over there."

"What was happening" was the burgeoning punk rock scene, which John witnessed with a mixture of fascination, amusement, and contempt. The clubs were overflowing with sneering kids in black leather, with razor blades and skinheads and spiked hairdos, all clamoring for bands like the Sex Pistols, the Clash, Generation X. The prevailing attitude was to dismiss violently anything even remotely connected to the rock establishment—rock stars like Rod the Mod, with fancy managers like Billy Gaff, who drove Rolls Royces and wore purple velvet, were held up to ridicule, condemned as self-indulgent, irrelevant fops and dandies. And John, as a member of the Riva organization, would soon be accorded the same treatment.

"I respected the statement they were making," John says of the punk movement, "but I couldn't *believe* it. The astonishing thing to me was the way they behaved as if their lives depended on it. It seemed real pretentious. I mean, Iggy Pop was *real,* and he'd been doing that stuff a long time ago. The Sex Pistols, to me, weren't real when I first saw them—it all seemed like just another haircut. Iggy was the definitive punk person, the constant upheaval of oneself, always searching, always confused, angry, outrageous. The Clash, the Stranglers, they seemed too calculating . . . There was no way I was going to jump on that bandwagon."

John nonetheless made the rounds of the clubs with hs friends, checking out the music. One night he went to the Vortex, one of the more feral and dangerous of the punk clubs, with Mick Ronson and Lee Black Childers. "Ronson got run out of the place!" John laughs. "It was like culture clash: He was wearing this satin jacket and they gave him so much shit about it that he finally had to leave. These were big mothers with pins sticking through their ears . . . We stayed and watched Sham 69 playing with about five other bands. It was frightening!"

It was becoming painfully clear to John that he didn't fit in with the rock establishment—the record companies, the managers, the press, etc.—and he didn't quite fit in with the kids either. Moreover, the punks had provided him with a graphic object lesson in the continuing innate power of rock & roll but sharply contrasted with what he saw as its fickleness, its hypocrisy—for no sooner was the punk movement born than it was rapidly institutionalized, commercialized, swallowed whole by the very establishment it was designed to subvert. "I started questioning the whole rock and roll reality at that time," he says. "I guess it was just the beginning of an awareness for me: You couldn't fulfill the expectations of the industry, couldn't fulfill the expectations of the kids; the only thing you could do was be true to yourself."

The British music press wasted no time setting on Johnny Cougar like a pack of grinning jackals. The *New Musical Express,* that stolid arbiter of musical fashion then worshipping at the altar of Elvis Costello, called the

"Why is this well-dressed man so angry?"

songs on *A Biography* "as weak as pressurized shandy," the lyrics "pretty weary," and his voice "Bob Seger with throat problems." "Perhaps you've seen those Cougar posters lining the walls of the tubes," noted Marcus Smith in the *West London Observer*. "I thought the lad was modeling a new line in suits . . . after hearing the record, perhaps modeling might be better suited . . ." And so on. John became immediately defensive and surly—what the British call "bloody-minded"—and would give the press tit-for-tat. What developed was a running feud between Cougar and Fleet Street. Referring to the "stroppy lyrics and cover photo" during an interview, journalist Murray Gammick queried, "Why is this well-dressed man so angry?"

"Why am I *angry?* Because I have to put up with a bunch of fucking idiots all the time like you! You are so caught up in the fucking hip world, you make me *sick*. Well dressed? That coat cost me four dollars! You wouldn't know well dressed if it came up and bit you on the dick! And don't ask me about the record because I'm sure that every record you have in your collection, you don't have a fucking *clue* what they're about anyway . . ."

The truly miraculous thing about "I Need a Lover" was how well it did on the British charts after its release, considering the field of negative energy that seemed to surround Johnny Cougar in England. The week of July 21, 1978, saw the record at No. 17; the album's other single, "Factory," didn't do nearly as well, reaching No. 34. The singles were accompanied by a pair of video clips designed to promote them on shows like "Old Gray Whistle Test," which were the British equivalent of *American Bandstand*. The clips were rudimentary—"I really didn't understand what video was all about, didn't know what the hell I was doing," John says—yet it was clear that he was *videogenic,* in the truest sense of how the word was coming to be applied to artists who would make the most natural use of this nascent medium. Years before the advent of MTV, he was gaining experience that would later prove invaluable to his career.

For the time being, however, there was nothing left to do but head out on the road. A series of tours were booked with John as an opening act throughout England and the continent. In March, he and the band opened for John Miles, playing such places as the Apollo in Glasgow, Colston Hall in Bristol, the Hammersmith Odeon in London, and the Hippodrome in Birmingham. "People absolutely ignored us," John recalls. "We never got booed off, but we could tell that they hated us. It hurt our morale, but it certainly taught me how to play in front of a hostile audience!" "There were places in the northern parts of England where literally nobody showed up," adds Tim Elsner, who'd come over to help. "In Glasgow, he was determined to walk out there with an acoustic guitar and play 'Taxi Dancer,' and people would be screaming at him to play rock and roll. He had to back off."

The shows didn't go much better on the continent, where they opened for Nazareth and Blue Oyster Cult throughout Germany, France, Sweden, and Belgium. "It wasn't too bad when we played with Nazareth in Germany," remembers Larry Crane. "A lot of American servicemen came to see us, and we went over pretty good with them. But playing with Blue Oyster Cult was horrible. We *hated* those guys."

After nine months, John was beginning to lose patience. The days found him more and more irascible in his moods, more combative. "He was frustrated because he felt things weren't moving fast enough for him," Tim Elsner explains. "And he wasn't totally convinced that what Billy Gaff was doing was the right thing. He felt handcuffed; he wasn't making any money and Gaff was calling all the shots. They'd have some serious arguments on the phone."

Just as things seemed bleakest, news arrived that "I Need a Lover" had gone No. 1 in Australia. All of a sudden, John was considered a "star" down under, even if he couldn't get himself arrested in Great Britain or the United States. Plans were put together for a whirlwind promotional visit. "When we arrived at the hotel I was staying at in Melbourne," says John, "a bunch of kids—about four hundred—were in front of the hotel. I asked, 'Who's staying here?' and Gaff answered, 'You are!' "

The tour would not pass without incident, however. "I Need a Lover" had received a great deal of lipservice from Molly Melbourne, Australia's version of Dick Clark, who invited John to be a guest on his TV show almost as soon as he arrived. "Most of the music shows over there—and in Europe—seem pretty corny to an American," remarks John. "They're really kind of like *Sesame Street* with rock and roll." Following his stint on television, John was interviewed in his hotel room, and somebody asked, "How did it feel being on the show?" Tired from jet lag and two straight weeks of promotion and the fifteen other interviews that day, John responded, "Ah, you know, I thought it was pretty stupid . . ."

Well, the comment found its way to the cover of national magazines. Molly was incensed and promptly penned an article, "Johnny Cougar Bares His Immature Claws" for the Australian version of *TV Guide*. The general consensus in Australia was one of wounded outrage: Here was this little jerk displaying the temerity and bad taste to put down the very show that broke his record! "I called Molly and apologized," John says. "He was only mad at me for about two days, but the incident didn't do much for my reputation."

All in all, John considers the eleven months spent abroad as among the most hapless of his life. He was homesick, disoriented, and even more angry than when he'd arrived in England. His single accomplishment was a song that at least had made some waves for him, but America still knew nothing of "I Need a Lover." Finally Jeff Franklin of ATI put together a deal with Mercury-Phonogram in Chicago, and John Mellencamp would have at least one more shot at a legitimate career in America. He packed up his family and band and headed for home, nervous, roiling with frustration, and determined not to blow it again. "I also made another resolution," he says. "This *Johnny* shit simply *had* to go . . ."

III

JOHN COUGAR

Or, I Need a Lover Who'll Sit on My Face

Alright. I'm going to do something you'd never
thought I'd do onstage. I'm going to a bit now that
I was arrested for. I'm going to tell you the
dirtiest word you've ever heard onstage. It is
just *disgusting!*
   —Lenny Bruce, "The Dirty Word Concept"
      The Essential Lenny Bruce

Your magazine is very good about
picking up on the new acts in town, but
there's one person you've missed—that's
rocker John Cougar. He's very cute and
he has a new LP out now. I'd appreciate
any info you can give me.
      —letter to *Sixteen Magazine*
         September 1980, signed
         Kathy Buhrer
         Belpre, Kansas

Look, I'm a second-level guy, not a star . . .
I'm not really John Cougar, you know.
I'm John Mellencamp from Seymour, Indiana,
who used to pour concrete.
      —John Cougar to Dennis Hunt
         Los Angeles Times
         December 7, 1980

No sooner had John returned to the States than he heard the startling news
that Phil Spector wanted to produce his next record. Boy genius producer of
the 1960s, creator of the immortal wall of sound, Phil Spector was the
impresario of the great girl groups like the Ronettes and the Crystals, the man
behind such classics as "You've Lost That Lovin' Feelin' " and "River Deep,

(Photos by Norman Seeff)

"I Need A Lover"

"Small Paradise"

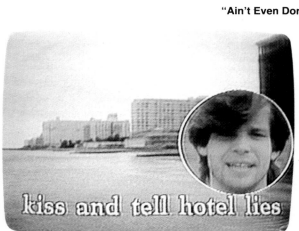

"Ain't Even Done With the Night"

kiss and tell hotel lies

"Miami"

"Hand To Hold Onto"

VIDEO

"Hurts So Good"

"Jack and Diane"   **"Crumblin' Down"**

"Pink Houses"

GALLERY

Mountain High." Excited, John went over to his house in Los Angeles, past the heavy double doors, into a dark, gothic mansion, for an encounter with rock's most legendary recluse and madman. "The living room was big enough to play football in," recalls John, "and I waited for about two hours. All of a sudden I felt this tap on my shoulder and there he was—it was like he came out of some trapdoor or something. I almost jumped out of my skin! He was dressed up like a Lord, and he wore this strange-looking wig, kind of falling off the side of his head . . ."

"I liked that record you did in England," Spector told him, "and I wanna produce your next album here, only I wanna cut that same album, see, only do it *my* way. It'll be fabulous, unbelievable, a classic, I got it all figured out, exactly what I'm gonna do, you're gonna *love* it . . ."

It went on like this for hours, Spector verbally browbeating him and John patiently trying to explain that he'd written a whole new crop of songs for his next record and only wanted to use a couple of songs from the last one because nobody had heard them in America yet, to which Spector would giggle in his strange way and say, "Great, that's great," and just go on and say the same thing over again.

The tirade went on, with Spector telling him he was the only one who could ensure him his rightful place in the pantheon of rock's great immortals, but as the producer became more shrill, trying to intimidate him, John became nervous. Of course, Spector's eccentricity was legendary—"I figured all geniuses are mad, right?" John said—but as time passed John began to see less method in the man's madness. "I wanted to get out of there. I said, 'Look, I gotta go back to my hotel room for a while, take care of a few things, okay?' He said, 'All right, do what you have to do, then come on back here. I've got dinner planned. We've got lots to talk about.' It was like walking out of the house that Gloria Swanson lived in on *Sunset Boulevard,* back into the real world. As soon as I opened the door to my room, the phone was ringing. It was Spector. 'Where are you? We're having dinner, I'm sending my bodyguard to get you.' He was after me! I just got on a plane and flew out of town . . . It was funny, I guess, but I was freaked!"

Back in Indiana, John found himself a new guitar player to add to the band: Mike Wanchic, who'd played on his original Bloomington demos and had since been playing with singer/songwriter Randy Handly. Wanchic was a specialist of the thin Stratocaster/Telecaster school of rock guitar, a good-looking ex-hippie from Kentucky who'd grown up on the same radio stations as John. The band called him "Chief" because he once lived in a tepee and loved the natural, outdoor life—he delivers his own children. Wanchic was a real rock & roll romantic. "John was volatile in those days," he says. "A lot of people couldn't work with him—you had to be very level-headed. He was hard to please, kind of like General Patton. If he didn't say anything, you knew you were doing okay."

Wanchic managed to injure his new boss during the recording of the album. "We were at the beach," he says, "and John and Larry decided they were going to throw me in the water—you know, one, two, three, heave-ho!—only I grabbed John's hand and took him with me. He flipped onto his left shoulder and broke it. He was in agony for the next six weeks! Boy, I sucked some serious swamp gas for that little number . . ."

The game plan for the record reflected John's growing need to begin carving a niche for himself. "I just decided to stop trying to be John Cale, because nobody was taking me seriously anyway," he says. "It seemed that critics were never going to like me, and it was too late to be the Next Big Thing. The thing I wanted to do was just learn how to write melodies and get myself on the radio and make some kind of a career for myself . . ."

Studio time was booked at Criteria in Miami, Florida. The producers finally engaged for the record were Ron and Howard Albert, veterans of Firefall, the Allman Brothers, and McGuinn, Clark and Hillman. "They were nice guys, but they didn't really have a handle on who we were," Larry Crane says. "They were in a real Miami kind of cool groove, kind of behind the times. That record wasn't fun to make at all." Mike Wanchic agrees: "They were the *wrong* choice for the album. They seemed more interested in going to their fishing classes in the evening than in what we were trying to do. We brought in this Dire Straits record, to show them the kind of stuff we liked, and Howard Albert said, 'If *that's* a hit, I'll quit the record industry.' It was 'Sultans of Swing.' "

Largely because John was now trying to concentrate on writing songs around simple melodies with hooks, his producers aimed for the cleanest, most commercial sound possible. The result was that, on *John Cougar,* his ballads were overproduced, with too much orchestration; and the leaner, more hard-edged songs were sanitized with piano and slick arrangements that did little to enhance the material. The problem was simple: John simply did not yet know his way around the studio and was unhappily realizing that the songs were not coming out the way he heard them in his head. He was frustrated, disaffected; it was a time when the producers and studio staff, exposed to his uneven moods, started saying, "That John is a *little bastard*"—and the sobriquet would stick. But there was one lucky development: John met Don Gehman, the brilliant young engineer who had designed

(Norman Seeff)

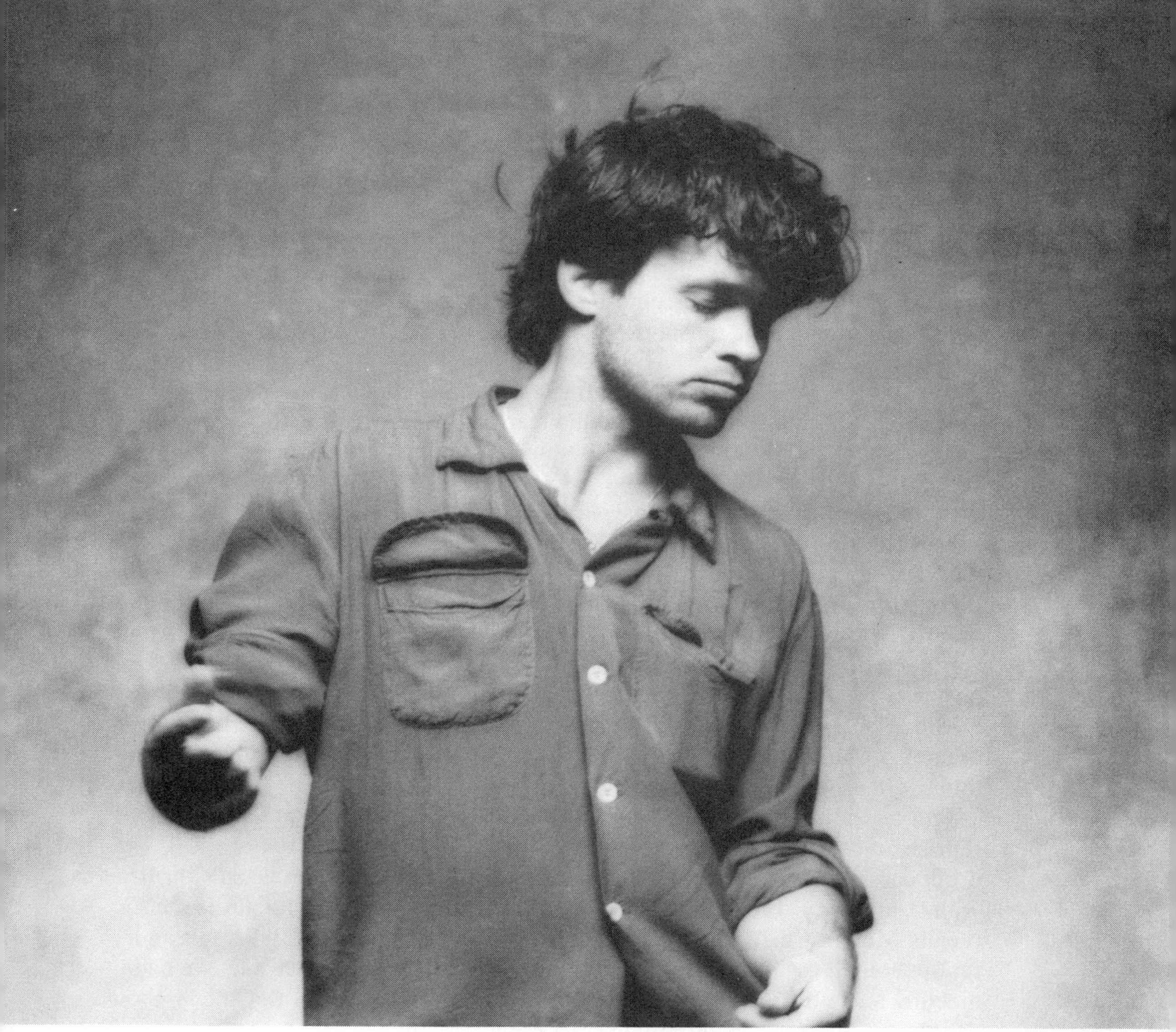

Criteria—an easygoing technician with a natural, intuitive sense of music, who started demystifying the studio for John and would eventually help him take control of his own sound.

The songs of *John Cougar* were a mixed bag of old and new, with lyrics that showed a growing preoccupation with sex, love, and social observation. "Miami," recorded with the Cuban rhythm section "Foxy," was a bit of funk about the local scene and the girls ("Well, they are easy to look at, they are hard to hold"); "Small Paradise" described a steamy doorway tryst of "two veteran lovers" as "a neon sign blinks outside in the pouring rain." The song was built around their kiss, a gesture that displays what was becoming a prevalent attitude in John's music: "Well, it ain't love but it ain't bad." The album was filled with lust and good-time girls ("Chinatown," "Sugar Marie") and the simple need to get out and strut ("Night Dancin' "). In "Pray For Me," the drama of the music is offset by the humor of the lyrics:

> Well, Shakespeare threw down his pencil
> Said I think I'm gonna start layin' brick
> Too much of this Romeo stuff enough to make
> Anybody sick

The LP also contained a new version of "Taxi Dancer," lushly produced, with the vocals backed up and spliced together from chorus to verse—still pretty, but unfortunately without the organic power and spontaneity of the original. However, the other main ballad, "The Great Midwest," represented another songwriting breakthrough for John—a simple, unvarnished social portrait of his roots. "Don't get me wrong I ain't complainin'," he sings about mediocrity in the Midwest, the machismo, the compromises, the busted dreams, "I ain't braggin' nor do I mean to place blame/That's just the way things are around here."

The big hope for a single was a truncated, pop-oriented, much-belabored reprise of "I Need a Lover"; out of the $70,000 budget for the LP, the producers probably spent the lion's share on this song. "John wasn't thrilled with it, and they'd gone through so much time and expense to recut the song," recalls Martin Cerf, who was by then working promotion for Riva, "and I really thought the original was better. About a month before release, we had a meeting and Billy Gaff agreed. Ron and Howard Albert were mortified—they couldn't believe we wanted to scrap their version. It was a tooth-and-nail battle for three days . . ."

As the package for the album was put together, John began to assert

himself—his pretty boy image was gone forever. "It had obviously been
uncomfortable for him with MainMan," Cerf points out, "and the same thing
had failed in London, so Billy developed the good sense to let Mellencamp be
Mellencamp." Norman Seeff, the South African expatriate physician, who
had come to America to become perhaps the most stylish, sought-after
photographer of music people during the 1970s, was hired to do the album.
Seeff's shootings were no mere photo sittings, but actual encounter sessions
many hours long, during which the subjects, in hundreds of rapid-fire expo-
sures, were encouraged to reveal themselves through movement, behavior,
psychodrama. The image that John selected for the cover perfectly expressed
his mood at the time: an extreme close-up of a tough, insolent, stubble-faced
kid, smoking a cigarette right in your face. The photo does not ask for
acceptance; on the contrary, it seems to dare you to knock the cigarette out of
his mouth and challenge him to a fight. He would have little difficulty finding
people to pick up the gauntlet.

For one thing, the people at Mercury did not seem any more inclined to like
John Cougar than MCA had. Cerf approached the company with an aggressive promotional campaign for the record all drawn up. Jeff Franklin at the
ATI booking agency was lining up a twenty-city tour, and Gaff had fronted the
money for videos of two songs—"Small Paradise" and "Miami"—both of
them produced by Simon Fields and directed by Bruce Gowers. "Small

Paradise'' begins with the feet of the lovers approaching each other on the street, then locking in the embrace as the camera wanders into a sleazy club, where John performs the song; "Miami" was a combination travelogue of the Gold Coast and an anthem to Tits and Ass On The Beach—kind of early *Miami Vice,* with the words to the choruses rolling onscreen, complete with the bouncing ball of John's face singing them. Mercury was unimpressed and refused to put up money, however. "I freaked out and called Billy," Cerf recalls. "He said, 'Don't worry. We'll do it ourselves.' There was no way Billy was going to go out and fight for an unknown kid like John Cougar the way he had fought for Rod Stewart ten years earlier, yet he was willing to *invest* in John—he knew he'd get the money back somewhere down the line. Billy didn't see John as a superstar, but as a potential success." "What Billy saw in John was an arrogance—that fight instinct," explains Russel Shaw, another Riva employee who would work closely with John on subsequent albums and tours. "Those are the ones he's attracted to because he thinks they have what it takes to go all the way."

"I Need a Lover" was destined to launch two careers. Shortly before the release of *John Cougar,* Mike Chapman contacted the Riva people about using the song for an unknown singer named Pat Benatar, whose debut album he was about to produce. The song hadn't panned out for Suzy Quatro, but Chapman hadn't been able to get it out of his mind. When he requested a tape of the song for Benatar, she received not Punter's original but the discarded Albert version done at Criteria and she modeled her rendition very faithfully on the tape. Even though her version is considerably more tame, the lyrics of the song, coming from a tough little female, seemed audacious—a neofeminist statement. When released, her single received tremendous airplay, propelling her first album, *In the Heat of the Night,* to sales of over eight hundred thousand.

Ironically, the Cougar "Lover" only reached No. 20 on the charts, yet it achieved a kind of album-oriented radio (AOR) cult status almost immediately. Bill Hard of the *Friday Morning Quarterback* tip sheet remembers picking the song out of the box as one that would travel far, despite the fact that it came out of left field. "Like most records that break by unknown artists without great promotional expenditures, it was a function of a few stations adding it and people starting to talk," Hard says. "In this case, the long, instrumental introduction actually helped the record by singling it out. Cougar also had that rough-cut boyish appeal."

At WMMS, which had first played "Chestnut Street" to no response years before, Kid Leo felt that his initial belief in Cougar as an artist had been confirmed. " 'I Need a Lover' became huge in Cleveland," he says. "Actually, we didn't hardly even play Benatar's version here because John's became so popular."

After the release of the album, John Cougar received his very first favorable notices in the music press. "Cougar's music is tough and contemporary," opined *Billboard,* "while his voice has the command and character to complete the package." *Cashbox* ventured that "John Cougar deserves to come back." Even so, "Small Paradise" and "Miami" sank quickly when they were released, and there were bad reviews right alongside the good ones. The *New Times Weekly* called the record "pedestrian rock built around Springsteen overtones"; the *Bee* of Fresno, California, accused Cougar of directly plagiarizing Bob Seger's "Night Moves" for "Chinatown": "Something seems carefully cultivated about the three-day growth on his cheeks and the length of that cigarette," wrote Eric C. Strom in that paper. "Like the potboiling studio photographs of impeccably grizzled actors portraying Basque sheepherders, is John Cougar playing at being a rock & roller?"

Undoubtedly, John had at least satisfied his most modest goals with the record. "We're not anywhere near home free," he told Scott Puhl of the Lansing, Illinois, *Sun Journal.* "I've sold a lot of records this time, about 150,000 albums. That's not a lot compared to what a lot of people do, but it's enough to be able to support the band another year, and the record company has recouped all their money."

People would now come up to him and ask, "Hey John, how come you're doing Pat Benatar's song?"—to which John would laugh and say, "Because I like it!"

There was nothing left to do but hit the road.

Now calling his band the Zone, John added a keyboardist named Eric Rosser—"Doc," as he was called—a classical musician from Indiana University who auditioned for the group by glibly tinkling out some flawless Floyd Cramer–style piano. Eccentric, offbeat, and very professorial-looking with his beard and spectacles, the sight of Doc onstage made it obvious that the Zone was not the normal rock band; they weren't punk, and they certainly weren't heavy metal. "Nobody knew what to make of us," says Mike Wanchic. "We were some serious backwoods-type boys, completely green to the big time, out on the road with an English road crew. We did every club in the country . . ."

John hit the road with an iron-willed determination to put himself across. His attitude had changed since England. Rule No. 1: Don't take yourself so seriously! He explained his new performing philosophy to *Rocks Off:* "Let's get our priorities straight: When it comes down to getting laid or listening to some guy singing songs, you know what's gonna happen and who's gonna get laid . . . If I can create an evening of whoopin' and hollerin' and help somebody get laid, that's what I like to do!''

There were still occasions when he never even got a chance onstage. In Oakland, John and the Zone were added at the very last minute as the opening act for Richie Blackmore and Rainbow. The audience was a rabid, rowdy heavy-metal crowd, some so stoned on Quaaludes that they were throwing up on themselves or shooting Mace at each other; the lap of the stage was infested with some particularly bloodthirsty-looking Hell's Angel types. A dangerous enough situation was only made worse by the fact that the crowd was under the mistaken assumption that the heavy-metal act Judas Priest was going to be the opener. The lights dimmed, and the band heard the hoarse, terrifying chants of *Judas Priest! Judas Priest!* When the emcee announced "Ladies and gentlemen, John Cougar and the Zone!" the band was greeted with a hail of debris. "I thought we'd better do a song they knew," John says, "so we opened with 'I Need a Lover.' " *Wrong move.* "It started raining spit," Larry Crane says. "Ferd was covered with it! It was disgusting . . . They were throwing everything they could get their hands on. We played three songs and ran off. That was the first and last time we were ever booed off a stage."

In Duluth, John found himself in an identical predicament: ten thousand screaming maniacs thought he was going to be Judas Priest, only this time he was not about to capitulate so easily. "We came out to ten thousand boos, and all of a sudden the shit starts whizzing by us," relates Mike Wanchic. "But this time John really went after them; he worked his ass off. By the end of the show we had *every* one of those fuckers in our pockets." It was the beginning of a turnaround in John Cougar's live show. "It really taught me that it all came down to me as to whether or not we were going to get over," John says. "At that point, I really started to like the challenge."

From that moment on, John Cougar became virtually unstoppable on a concert stage. His shows quickly developed a reputation for humor, endless energy, unbridled profanity, and an instant rapport with his audiences. "We knew we weren't going to just stand there and blow people away with our artistry," says Larry Crane, "so we just decided to start enjoying ourselves. We did things just for shock's sake." The show now featured cover versions of the Skyhook's "You Only Like Me Because I'm Good in Bed," Honky Tonk Women," Van Morrison's "Domino," "Land of 1,000 Dances," and a blaring encore of Iggy's "Search and Destroy." John would bound acrobatically up onto Wanchic's shoulder, microphone in hand, and do numbers while the guitarist piggybacked him around stage. "John would wear those old jeans of his," Wanchic says, "and many times he'd rip clear through the crotch. He never wore underwear and his balls would be hanging out, so he'd run off stage and the roadies would duct-tape him back together and back out he'd go! He'd go crazy out there, climbing thirty to forty feet up the PA stacks. The production guys would be screaming 'Hey, get the fuck off there!' "

The production crew weren't the only people hurling imprecations at John Cougar. Once his shows started clicking into high gear, the headlining acts became wary of him. One by one, he began upstaging them, stealing their thunder, and it usually didn't matter who they were: Ian Hunter, Robin Trower, R.E.O. Speedwagon, Kiss. The tension was exacerbated by the old Bad Mellencamp Family Attitude—John hated many of the acts he had to open for. The Knack, then being touted as the Next Big Thing, were incensed when John added a hilarious parody of their hit "My Sharona" to his show—which quickly disqualified him, of course, from working with them. He didn't last long as the opener for Kiss either, with their fog clouds and shooting flames. "Kiss had these elaborate runways that went out thirty feet into the crowd," Mike Wanchic recalls, "and we were forbidden to use them. John would say, 'Oh, no problem,' and then thirty seconds into the show he'd go running right down one. One night we got out there and they were barricaded with this huge pile of chairs. John just kicked them down and went right on . . ."

At New York's Bottom Line, on November 11, 1979, John became a headliner by default when Tracy Nelson simply failed to show up for the second night of the booking. At Detroit's Centerstage later that month, he received thirteen stitches in his head after colliding with Mike Wanchic's guitar during the intro of "I Need a Lover." "Mike spun one way and John spun another," Larry Crane says, "and he got coldcocked right in the forehead! He put his hand up and, as soon as he saw the blood, he went right down. Billy Francis slung him over his shoulder like a sack of potatoes and carried him off."

Everywhere he went, he smoked and cursed incessantly during his performances. At the Starwood in Los Angeles, where the band did a live broadcast, one of the network engineers had to entreat him, "Do me a favor and hold it down with the *motherfuckers,* okay, kid?"

"Let me shoot it to you straight," Cougar told the *Desert News* during the tour. "Things haven't been moving too fast, but that's okay. What we want is longevity. We want to be making records for years."

That year, John made the first substantial sum of money in his career: royalties from Benatar's version of "I Need a Lover." "All of a sudden I had forty thousand dollars in my hands, and I didn't know what to do with it," he says, "so I called my Dad in Seymour and asked him if I should blow the money like I do everything else. He said, 'You'd better buy a house because one of these days this thing is going to be over and at least you'll have some place to live.'"

When John Cougar and the Zone made their first appearance on Dick Clark's *American Bandstand,* they performed "I Need a Lover" and "Small Paradise." Like hundreds of other acts before them, they dutifully lipsynched the words to the songs on camera, only Ferd was playing an upright bass and holding it like a guitar; the words John sang to the song were really "I Need a Lover Who'll Sit on My Face." During "Small Paradise," Doc gave the camera the middle finger, and during the obligatory few moments of questions, as if by way of explanation, John told Dick Clark, "We're just a bunch of hillbillies who don't know how to act." It was a bit of a goof, rock theater of the absurd. As John puts it, "We didn't care what anybody thought—we thought it was funny."

Almost from the beginning of his return to America, John Cougar was beset with public relations problems—"image related confusion," in the words of publicist Howard Bloom—that were partly a holdover from the MainMan days but were inflamed by new attitudes and situations. For one thing, he almost immediately offended people in the music business when Riva brought out a privately published book called *Trendsetters: John Cougar's Illustrated Salute to the Music Business*. The book was the brainchild of Gaff and Martin Cerf, designed as a promotional supplement for the album. What Cerf did was simply choose a number of prominent individuals from all aspects of the industry, photograph them, and collect them into a book.

The idea backfired: "I had no earthly idea that it was a *promotional* item," related tipster Bill Hard, who was included in the volume. "People who were left out were offended, and others felt 'Who the hell is *John Cougar* to be picking the trendsetters anyway?" (Of course, John had nothing to do with picking the actual subjects.) The book invited contempt because it seemed that John was kissing the asses of the very people who were in a position to further his career; which was, of course, precisely the idea of the project.

Far more upsetting, however, was the prevailing view that he was nothing more than a pallid, contrived ripoff. "The problem with John Cougar," pronounced *Melody Maker* at the time, "is that he wants to be Bruce

Springsteen, Tom Waits, and James Dean—and he isn't even Ricki Lee Jones." The elite of the music media, centered in New York and Los Angeles, who already deified Bruce Springsteen as the most preeminent rock poet and performer since Dylan, summarily dismissed John Cougar as blatantly derivative, quickly deducing that Cougar drew upon his Indiana roots and his adolescence just as Springsteen did the losers and pitstops of the Jersey Shore. But beyond their broad thematic similarities and the fact that their voices fell loosely into the category of the Mitch Ryder School of Gravel-Gargling Belting, the likenesses abruptly ended. Even at this early stage in Cougar's development, he *sounded* different from Springsteen. Still, the unfavorable comparisons would cling to him for years, casting a giant

John Cougar encounters the rock press.

shadow, providing the lofty example by which he would be forced to measure his own accomplishments.

In the beginning, the comparisons made John defensive, to the point that he denied so much as even listening to Springsteen's music, which he genuinely admired. As time passed, however, he became more secure about his own music, and his attitudes about the situation evolved from stoical acceptance ("Here's the bottom line," he told Dennis Hunt of the *LA. Times,* "I'd rather be compared to Springsteen than to Foreigner") to humor ("All that stuff they wrote about me, they missed the truth. The truth is, I always wanted to be Ronnie Van Zandt!").

Years later, after the comparisons had died down, John would meet the Boss for the first time backstage at the Market Square Arena in Indianapolis. "I really liked your last album," Springsteen graciously told him, "especially that song 'Pink Houses.' " "Hey, Bruce, you know I steal everything from you," John said with a big, wry grin on his face, which made Springsteen break up laughing and put his arm around John like an older brother.

From his reactions to the press, it was also becoming evident that John Cougar himself had no notions of ever wanting to become a "rock star" in the usual sense. "I'm not into thinking I'm cool because I make records," he told *Hot Potato* in December 1980. "I can show you a *Billboard* sheet—150 albums came out in the last month, and this month 50 of them are on the charts. It's no big deal having a record on the charts. Last year, 'I Need a Lover' was one of millions of songs on the charts!"

Rock stars had become paragons of pretentiousness to him—overblown, overpraised cultural icons who were completely removed from the concerns of the common man. "A lot of them don't know a damn thing about rock and roll. Just because you have ten bracelets on your arm doesn't make you a rock and roll star! We've got all the rock stars we need. We need real people who write songs to deal with real people who have real problems."

Such statements reflected John Cougar's growing populist attitudes about music. As an American historical tradition, populism embodies the common man's deepseated distrust of big-city slickers, big money, government, power, pretense. As a Midwesterner and a small town rebel, John felt a natural kinship with this most basic attitude, but began to apply it to the musical establishment, and to the way he felt about music. "Emotion has to do with rock and roll," he told interviewers, "that's what rock is about. It's immediate. You should hear it, feel it, and then forget it. It's nothing you *ponder . . .*" Even as his own music began to achieve critical acceptance in the years to come, he would stubbornly cling to this value. When asked what he really thought of other people's music, he'd be glad to tell you: not much. The Clash, critical darlings of the New Wave, were "pretentious": "Where do these bands get off thinking they know everything that's going on in South America or whatever? Did they go talk to the people there? I mean 'Know Your Rights' . . . Give me a break!" As for "progressive music" in general, "The only progressive band around is the Rolling Stones."

These remarks made good copy, but they would continuously get John into trouble. He would toss them off casually at odd moments, and if he didn't have two hours to explain himself, they would always get misconstrued. "He makes a writer's job easy because he's an ever-flowing source of free-spirited quotes," reported the *Birmingham News,* "but then he always has to accent them with a —— or an ——. It messes everything up because the only way to get around it in a family newspaper is use these ——'s, which takes all the fun out of it."

"Hey, I'll take a shot at anybody," John Cougar told the Knight Newspaper Service. "Basically, I don't give a (*bleep*). I mean, I do give a (*bleep*), but I don't give a (*bleep*), you know what I mean?"

One reason that John Cougar didn't give a (*bleep*) was that he had fallen hard for a twenty-year-old girl in Los Angeles, an experience that was shaking his life to the roots. Her name was Victoria Granucci, and she was the daughter of a veteran Hollywood stuntman named Phil Adams. Vicky's parents had divorced when she was very young, and she had grown up in Burbank. With long ash-blond hair and striking azure eyes, she was the absolute apotheosis of a California beauty, the sort of girl that John Mellencamp had dreamed about in high school. Most men, in fact, carry around within them an image of a girl who they've always imagined as perfect for them—the seed of the vision is planted during adolescence and takes shape with remarkable precision over the years and never quite goes away. Of course, very few men are lucky enough to actually *find* these girls, but on the day that John Cougar stopped at Billy Gaff's house, walking quickly through the living room, and saw Vicky seated on the couch, he had to face the fact that he had really found her.

Alright, the inevitable question: With a wife and child, what was he doing "looking" in the first place? Suffice to say that the rock & roll life will tempt any man and strain any marriage, regardless of circumstances and character; John was not beyond succumbing to temptation, particularly considering that he had married at seventeen, ten years before. As his close friend Tim Elsner explains, "Cil was aware of it, but she just preferred not to deal with it. Girls were something that John had never grown out of. He was like a competitive,

Vicky Mellencamp, then and now.

diehard high school jock who just couldn't give up his favorite sport—and his favorite sport had *always* been girls.''

Vicky, who had gone to work for Gaff at Martin Cerf's behest, was friendly with Carol Maruyama, who was dating Jimmy Horowitz of the Riva organization. "Carol kept calling me and asking me to come out with them," Vicky recalls, "and she wouldn't take no for an answer. I got to the restaurant and there was Carol and Jimmy, and another couple, and John, and an empty chair . . .''

Of course, John had persuaded Carol to set the whole thing up, but that first dinner did not go well. Vicky did not want him to think she was one of those "easy" girls who frequently hung around Gaff's house, which had the reputation of being a sort of Hotel California. "There was this incredible tension throughout the meal," she says. "I was really attracted to him, but I felt like he had all these ideas, and even though he wasn't saying anything, I had to put my foot down.''

"Don't think that something's going to happen," she warned him, "that's not."

Completely smitten by her beauty, John wanted to at least leave some kind of lasting impression. "Is this your wine?" he asked, gesturing toward her glass. When she nodded, he took his cigarette and put it out in her glass with a sizzle. She stared at him. "That's real cool," she said with acid sarcasm. "That's real funny . . ."

After dinner they all went back to Gaff's house, and John and Vicky sat on the couch and talked through the night. He found her down-to-earth, stable, bright, remarkably mature for her age; she liked his strong personality and the fact that he was so different from all the wishy-washy guys in LA. ("he wasn't too bad to look at either"). "I think she hated my guts at first," John says, "because I tried to be Joe Cool with her and she saw right through it. She was so amazing, so beautiful, I didn't know what to say to her at first! After one night together, we were inseparable. After a week I realized that I was in *big* trouble . . ."

By the time John left town to prepare for his next album, he had told her everything about himself—his hopes, dreams, fears, loves, hates—everything, of course, except that he was married.

Call him a typically male reprobate, but until he could figure out what to do, John tried to keep both women unaware of each other. He still loved Cil and Michelle, of course, and the thought of hurting them made him miserable. Cil knew nothing of Vicky, but Vicky found out very fast about Cil. The next time John was in town, Carol Maruyama, upset by the affair that she had initiated, dropped the bomb at a restaurant by mentioning "Cil" and "Chelle"—all Vicky had to do was watch John's jaw fall open to know what was going on. "Which one is the wife," she asked pointedly, "and which one is the daughter?"

What followed was a nerve-wracking period of indecision, during which they carried on a long-distance relationship. "I remember telling Eric Rosser how I couldn't deal with it anymore," John says. "I said, 'This person Vicky is fucking up my life, my marriage—I'm never going to see her again.' Two days later I was on a plane going back to LA."

To her credit, Victoria Granucci decided from the outset to play the whole situation straight, right down the line. "Once I realized how we felt about each other, I realized that regardless of whether or not it caused a blowout, Cil had a right to know about me. There were suspicions anyway, and I was always thinking, if that had been *me* and I'd been married for ten years, how could *I* fight? I told John upfront that ideally, when everything came to a head, that if they did separate, I didn't want to be around for a couple of months. I didn't want him to leave one situation and step right into another. He was used to that domestic situation, and I was used to living alone; my attitude toward him was, 'Let's see if you can even handle it without her before you expect me to fill her shoes.' "

It took about a year after their meeting before Vicky consented to move to Bloomington. By that time, John had bought a three-story redwood house not far from Lake Monroe. Three days earlier, Cil Mellencamp had moved into her own apartment with Michelle, but not before telling John, "I hope your new girlfriend at least knows how to fill out a check—*you* don't!"

After so many years of standing behind John while he was struggling, it was only natural that Cil would feel discarded, betrayed—especially now that John was experiencing the first glimmers of success. "I couldn't deal with it too well at first," she says, "but as some time passed I began to realize that it wasn't something that happened overnight—and it didn't happen because of Vicky. For one thing, we both definitely had changed, not in the same direction. He'd become halfway successful, and I used to hate sitting at home. I wanted more for myself. After we talked it over and decided to separate, I realized that if it hadn't been Vicky, it would have been someone else . . ."

Vicky's appearance in John's life created awkwardness among his friends, too. "We saw Vicky as this blond homewrecker from Los Angeles at first," says Gary Boebinger. "Everybody around John felt strongly about Cil. As time went on, we grew to really love Vicky, too . . ." Feelings were split: Some, like Ted and Marilyn, immediately accepted Vicky; others did not. The biggest question was how Michelle was going to deal with the situation. "Michelle would come over and I'd have to leave and hang out at the mall," Vicky says. "I'd feel terrible: She'd come over and eat this meal that this witch—the other woman—had prepared for her, and then leave. John was trying to protect everybody else's feelings, and it wasn't working; he was tearing himself apart. I felt that living this way was going to raise more animosity than if Cil and I just met and talked about everything. When I told John I was going to talk to her, he freaked out. 'She won't talk to you!' "

"She just walked right into the property-management office where I was working," Cil recalls. "I couldn't believe she had the nerve to do it! I tried to ignore her at first and pretend she just wasn't there. It was very emotional but really quite civilized. She just wanted to explain how she felt about John and that she understood how I was feeling. She wanted me to know that she always wanted John to be there for Michelle and that she knew that I would always be a special part of his life. We made a pact to be really honest with

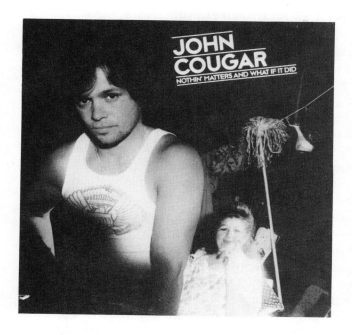

each other and really try to work things out, and we put our arms around each other and hugged. I felt a lot better afterward; I realized how glad I was that he was with somebody as nice as Vicky.''

When Vicky returned home, she found John in the throes of one of his major anxiety attacks. ''He was just sitting there, sweating,'' she remembers, ''in front of an ashtray filled with cigarette butts up to the ceiling.'' John needn't have worried; he was one of those extraordinarily lucky fellows to whom good fortune comes in the form of two good women.

''They became best friends, like two sisters,'' he marvels. ''It didn't take long before they were meeting each other for a glass of wine at the Firesign Inn!''

While the ballad of John and Vicky was being played out in Los Angeles and Bloomington, the LP *Nothing Matters and What If It Did* was recorded and released. The optimistic title came from an expression that Gary Boebinger was in the habit of using when he was feeling particularly gloomy and apathetic; John thought it aptly encapsulated his own attitude toward the record in general—at the time he was seriously considering chucking the whole music business and doing something else. Nevertheless, the album spawned two more chart singles, ''This Time'' and ''Ain't Even Done with the Night,'' which brought his career farther along toward radio viability, even if John himself prefers to forget the whole project.

From the outset, the album, which took three months to write and cost approximately $280,000 to produce, was rooted in chaos. For one thing, drummer Tom Knowles was fired before the band was about to head out to Cherokee Studios in Los Angeles. Knowles had learned that John had rewarded Larry Crane with a cash bonus for his guitar work on "I Need a Lover," and had angrily insisted on being given an equal sum. John tried to reason with him but the drummer threatened to walk if the money wasn't forthcoming; so John told him to "take a hike." Auditions were quickly held in Bloomington, and in walked Ken Aronoff of Worcester, Massachusetts, who had trained as a percussionist with the Boston Symphony Orchestra and had spent the last few years playing in a jazz fusion band around Bloomington. A bearded, beatnik type, he didn't know the first thing about rock drumming. "I walked in with about forty different cymbals and about a million drums," Aronoff says, "and the first thing John said was, 'Get rid of this, get rid of *that* . . .' I could tell he didn't like the look of me as soon as I walked in, but I played so hard I broke three sticks and cracked a cymbal in a matter of minutes. . . ." Aronoff was hired for the record, but not for long. "In *one hour* I was kicked off the record! I wasn't popular; everything I said was wrong. I was coming out of such a different musical bag—it was like running into a brick wall. John tried to send me home, but I wouldn't go; I wanted to stay and watch the two session drummers they hired." Letting Kenny Aronoff hang around and remain in the band turned out to be a fateful move; he would play a vital role on John's next record.

Initially, John had wanted *Nothing Matters* to be an album with an R&B feeling, so he engaged Steve Cropper to produce it. With his background as the guitarist with the legendary Booker T. and the MGs, writer of many Stax soul classics in Memphis during the 1960s (Eddie Floyd's "Knock on Wood," Wilson Pickett's "In the Midnight Hour"), Cropper seemed like the perfect choice. The only problem was that Cropper's mind was on Dan Ackroyd's and John Belushi's upcoming Blues Brothers project, which he was helping to organize. He worked on the album for only about four weeks, mostly during preproduction work, after which engineer Bruce Robb took over. Although it made the sound of the record uneven, the situation had some advantages: For one thing, Cropper's brief presence had influenced John's band ("We learned a lot about rhythm and tempo from him," says Larry Crane), and John, who actually produced parts of the record himself, realized that on his next LP he had to take command in the studio.

"This Time" represents John's first and only effort consciously to pen a commercial love song, much like Rod Stewart's "You're in My Heart." The

John cavorting with Edie Massey in "This Time."

words are obviously influenced by his relationship with Vicky ("I hope you don't lose that innocent laughter/I hope time doesn't take that away"); in fact, he had sent her a cassette of the song along with flowers and champagne when he first met her. The tune is a pleasant-enough pop confection, with Wanchic and Crane trading licks on the break, but "the first time I heard it on the radio, I almost puked," John says. "I decided *never* to try to write a formula song like that again."

The other single, "Ain't Even Done with the Night," came much closer to John's emerging style as a romantic but streetwise songwriter.

> Well, our hearts beat like thunder
> I don't know why they don't explode
> You got your hands in my back pockets
> And Sam Cooke's singin' on the radio . . .

The lyrics reveal a man quaking in his boots when his big romantic moment arrives—an honest glimpse into the experience of true love in the songwriter's own life.

> You say that I'm the boy who can
> Make it all come true
> Well, I'm tellin' you that I don't know
> If I know what to do . . .

Originally conceived as a good old-fashioned rock & roll song, the whole thing somehow got gussied up in the studio and transformed into another pop song, albeit a very catchy one, with hand claps on the refrains and a soaring sax solo.

If these two songs were conscious nods to the need for airplay and record sales, other songs on the album were aimed right at the censor. "Tonight," a funky, high-stepping ditty about the joyous lubricity a blue-collar worker feels for his woman during the day, could very well have been one of John's hottest songs had it not been for one X-rated line, involving a part of the female anatomy being applied to the fellow's face, that kept it off the radio. "We'd all been in a bad mood because we were in the studio so long, and everybody was tired of cutting that song, so I threw that line in there to liven things up," he explains.

As if that weren't bad enough, John then segued into a twenty-four-second bit of a capella harmony called "Cry Baby," in which a girl—"a top mechanic"—sits on his lap and plays with his "nuts and tool." "She'll do it, do it, do it, do it, do it, do it, do it," he sings. "She'll go down." These sexual references set up the outrageous, honkytonk "Wild Angel." Walking this fine line between romanticism and crassness would do little to endear him to feminists or critics who already considered him a macho lunkhead and a foulmouthed vulgarian. And in "Cheap Shot" he took on the whole music establishment—record companies, radio, critics, music media. "Initially it started as a joke," John says. "I wrote it at home and went into the studio and said to the band, 'How do you think the record company would feel about this song?' They all laughed . . . I didn't mean it to be that serious." The lyrics are a furious, suicidal indictment of the very institutions he most needed to promote his career. The worst backlash from the song came from indignant employees of his own record company. "Some thought it was funny, but most didn't appreciate it," John says. "I got my rear chewed out—phone calls in the middle of the night from somebody in the record company saying, 'I can't believe you said that about the company. We're down here in Tucson working our asses off for you and you're saying the record company stinks! You live in a nice home and drive Corvettes and Harley Davidsons. The record company has been *good* to you. Why are you being such a jackass?' "

"Toward the end of the record, I didn't even go to the studio," John confessed to the *Record*'s Deborah Frost in a 1983 article. "Me and the guys in the band thought we were finished, anyway . . . The worst thing was that I could have gone on making records like that for hundreds of years. Hell, as long as you sell a few records and the record company isn't putting a lot of money into promotion, you're making money for 'em and that's all they care about. Polygram loved *Nothing Matters*. They thought I was going to turn into the next Neil Diamond."

Reviews were mixed. *Modern Recording and Music* rated the performance as "wimpy," and the recording "obtuse": "It seems that Cougar, not unlike the month of March, had started out like a Cougar and now he's gone out like a goat." Many found the sexual songs tasteless, gratuitous; others liked the bright accessibility of "This Time" and "Ain't Even Done with the Night." Only the *Chicago Sun-Times,* calling John a "poet of the *real* world," weighed in with a rave, the very first of his career: "Spirit, spark and not a little smart-alecky sass—these are the essential ingredients of John Cougar's music . . . This record puts him right up there with those other rock & roll wizards, Costello and Springsteen."

The videos produced for the two singles fared much better, both of them clever visual renditions of the songs that helped attract attention. Once again working with producer Simon Fields and director Bruce Gowers, John utilized actress Edith Massey, who also graces the cover of *Nothing Matters,* for "This Time," a lighthearted, campy romp shot in black and white. The piece opens with a long white staircase, fringed with elegant, statuesque ladies. The Zone, a string quartet in white tails, accompanies John as he sings the song to the object of his adorations: Edie, best known for her portrayal of the Egg Lady in John Waters's *Pink Flamingos,* a mountainous hag of a woman looking preposterously wonderful in ostrich feathers and cigarette holder, her teeth a mass of black decay. Mike and Larry play their guitar solos on violins, and John and Edie dance off together dreamily through palm fronds. "This time I think I'm *really* in love . . ."

The "Ain't Even Done" video turned out to be the precise visualization of the feeling that John had originally intended for his music: a stylized interpretation of early 1960s rock & soul. The band is dolled up like the Temptations, all dancing in a line with those unmistakable soul gesticulations, while John runs into frame, hair slicked back, and grabs the microphone. With its white background, low camera angles, and freeze-frame and slow-motion editing, the piece plays havoc with visual perspective. In a truly inspired bit of lunacy, the sax solo is manically "talked" to the camera by Doc Rosser. At the end, John sends up one of his idols, James Brown, falling to his knees as the band wraps a cape around his shoulders. Both videos served notice that John Cougar possessed a very playful, mordant sense of rock & roll style.

The dance routine for the video worked like gangbusters when John performed the song on *American Bandstand;* the audience actually erupted in screams, leaving him googly-eyed with amazement. No such luck, however, when he did the song at the American Music Awards at the end of 1980. People at Polygram, along with Billy Gaff, had talked him into doing the show against his will: "You need the exposure—this is a nationally televised, prime-

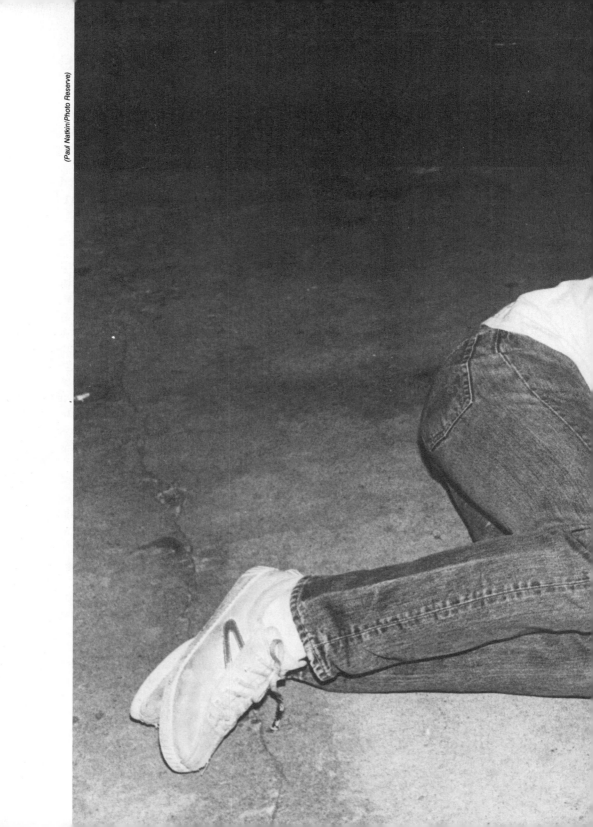

time broadcast!" John relented, and it was decided that he would do "Ain't Even Done with the Night," complete with the band in tails and the talking sax of Doc. John performed in blue jeans, V-neck sweater, and Bass Wee-juns—John Mellencamp, Seymour High, circa 1968. Nothing went right: He was so nervous he could hardly breathe, the floor was so slick that his feet kept sliding and he kept messing up the tightly rehearsed dance steps; the mike slipped away, and he sang in a strangulated tone of voice like he was on the verge of tears. His stage fright wasn't helped by the elegantly turned out people in the Shrine Auditorium of Pasadena, who sat in their chairs and gaped at him, not knowing quite what to make of it all. As it turned out, many were taken with the act and would remember it for a long time, but John thought it was a miserable bomb—total humiliation—shades of Johnny Cougar Day all over again. Back at the hotel, he fell into one of his marathon anxiety attacks—a flat-out, palpitating humdinger. "I was so bummed out," he remembers, "I had to go to Cedars-Sinai because I thought I was having a heart attack! That was the turning point for me. I decided if I'm not calling the shots, if I can't do it my way, I wouldn't do it at all."

John Cougar spent the next eight solid months on the road, opening for the Kinks, among other groups. It was a curious combination of bands, but one with good drawing power. John was developing a solid market in the Midwest, where the Kinks had more trouble selling tickets. He was thrilled to be on the road with a prestige act, not some mindless heavy-metal affair. The only problem was money. "We were getting, like, five hundred dollars a booking," he recalls. "We were losing six to seven thousand a week!" Over the course of that year, John Cougar lost between $200,000 and $300,000.

The act itself had evolved into a breakneck, pounding, macho display of Midwestern rock & roll—sometimes juvenile and bordering on bad taste. "When I look back on a lot of it now," John says, "it seems like I was doing a sort of Andy Kaufman routine—you know, wrestling women onstage, doing anything to get attention. I was in the best shape of my life at that point, and the bottom line was to get on the stage and go nuts, to have a good time."

Girls would sally forth to do battle with him during various numbers. John would sing, "She'll go down!" and take them down to the turf—which always turned the spectacle into a wild melée. The show now included X-rated versions of two classics, "Louie, Louie," and "Hang On, Sloopy." What's more, the band was an even more oddball-looking lot than before, what with Doc flailing madly away at his piano like a hopped-up Boris Karloff. "We were all at the Chateau Marmont in Los Angeles one night watching horror flicks," Mike Wanchic recalls. "It was a Lugosi–Boris Karloff film, and John looks at Eric and says 'That's for you!' So Doc went into the bathroom and shaved his head to a point! He wore it that way for the next year." Ken Aronoff had shaved his beard, and with his slightly balding pate and prominent proboscis—they called him the Schnozz—he was a cross between new wave and neobiblical. There was Larry Crane, still looking sixteen with his bouncing mane of red hair; and Ferd the bass player, bug-eyed and cadaverously thin in his paint-splattered suits; and Mike Wanchic, blue-eyed and cleft-chinned, handsome as a comic book superhero. The outfit was fronted by a five-foot-seven little package of nonstop manic energy, who would begin his shows by taking a deep drag on a cigarette backstage before exploding across the stage in a crazed series of acrobatic handsprings and cartwheels. Coming to a halt before the microphone, he would sullenly exhale a cloud of smoke into the spotlight and shout, "So what the fuck's goin' on!" After a performance at the University of Cincinnati Field House, *Creem*'s Richard Riegel described John Cougar as follows: "The Coug's dressed in slim black vest (his ever-ready pack of Marlboros nudging out of the pocket) and jeans, with sleeveless teeshirt underneath, to keep his bulging biceps free for easy product identification. Cougar's virtuoso neo-Hoosier hairdo and his pumping iron arms overshadow his trim little ass and legs, giving him mythic proportions up onstage; he suggests either a Brecht–Weill American roustabout antihero, ca. 1929, or maybe even the (distanced) country cousin of the macho man saluting from the back cover of Lou Reed's *Transformer.*"

Laughing, grimacing, diving onto the floor, hooting and howling his way through night after night, John was having the most fun of his life. "His onstage persona, as seen at the Bottom Line last week, is cut from the same cloth as Mitch Ryder, Eric Burdon, and other macho twits," Ed Naha remarked in a *Village Voice* review entitled "Mucho Macho." Noting that his music had little to do with "poetics," and that he came off as "somewhat of a sexist nerd," Naha observed that his antics "were delivered with such wide-eyed glee that very few people in the audience took offense. Well, at least no one threw anything at him . . . It's not so much the material as the power *behind* it—Cougar's personality—that impresses the listener . . . When you watch John Cougar perform, you have to leave your social consciousness and maybe even your IQ at the door, but you'll have a great time."

While the records were released, John's relations with his own record company remained volatile, except for a few individuals. The music business, after five years, had become another authority figure to rebel against—like his father, his school, the Seymour cops, and Tony DeFries had been. Around this time, Russel Shaw was assigned by Riva to work closely with John. "In those early days, he was a little madman with the record company," Shaw says. "His mind was always going; he'd never turn it off, except when he was on one of his motorcycles."

For one thing, John went around telling everybody how much he hated his record. "Every time he did an interview, he'd mention it," recalls Polygram publicist Sherry Ring Ginsberg. "It was like 'Hey, John, you're not supposed to *say* that about your own record!' But he did it anyway."

Nevertheless, the album was getting noticed. According to Bill Hard of the *Friday Morning Quarterback,* "Ain't Even Done with the Night" was "a step in the right direction. It was obvious that he was at least beginning to develop a style that he was comfortable with. That song started moving him into the category of a legitimate singer/songwriter."

At Polygram, radio promotion man Bill Cataldo began paying closer attention to John Cougar's career. " 'This Time' went half-assed as far as sales went," Cataldo recalls, "and the accounts were packing up all the albums for returns. Then after we released 'Ain't Even Done with the Night,' and we got halfway up the charts, they actually unpacked them and brought them out on the floors again and tried selling them. The album netted about three hundred thousand units and got him going a little bit." In the A&R department, Jerry Jaffe was also keeping his eye on Cougar. "After that album," Jaffee says, "we were in a great position because, while it didn't go that far, it managed to break down enough doors so that if the next one was in the groove, it might really fly."

In the mind of John Cougar, then pulling off the road and heading back to Indiana, he wasn't so sure there was even going to *be* a next one. "I was fed up with the whole business," he says. "I was thinking of quitting. I figured I probably had already made more money than I had a right to expect—I had a nice home, some bikes, a couple of cars—I *had* everything I could possibly want. At the time I didn't really give a shit if that was my last record."

IV

AMERICAN FOOL

Wherein Jack Meets Diane

Now that I'm gettin' older, so much older
I long for those young boy days . . .
—"Hurts So Good"

Can you believe that such a simple guy
can get into so much trouble?
—J. Cougar to Christopher Connelly
"Hey, John Cougar, What's Your Problem?"
Rolling Stone, Dec. 1982

Now, for virtually the first time since John Cougar had set out on his New York adventure six years earlier, he had a chance to step back and take stock of his surroundings. Compared to his old friends, he had the life of a country squire in Bloomington. Mark Ripley was married by that time, still living in Seymour with a couple of kids, scratching out a meagre living by selling shirts at Richarts Casual Shop. Gary Boebinger was still teaching English in Nashville, Indiana, scraping by with his family. Jay Nicholson, the friend who had been the inspiration for "I Need a Lover," had passed through some very hard times—heavy drugs, alcohol, suicidal despair—before becoming a born-again Christian and pulling himself together. When John attended his ten-year high school reunion, he discovered that one of his favorite girlfriends had married a wealthy man and become a sexually frigid socialite. Another friend had gone to prison for passing $22,000 worth of bad checks. Everywhere he looked, he saw paunches and receding hairlines and bored people who had settled into jobs they could just barely tolerate. None of these lessons were lost on John Cougar, who began to put them into their Midwestern context. Everything—family, friends, old lovers, the very streets and fields—suddenly became imbued with more meaning for him, viewed from the vantage point of someone turning thirty. "The thing about all these guys," explained John to Mark Rowland of *Musician,* "their lives just kind of ended at sixteen. 'Cause after that, people just gave up; in a town like Seymour, that's easy to do. And in a sense, that's what life's *really* about. All the stuff about going to school and getting a degree and everything turning out hunky-dory—it's bullshit. Reality isn't like that. It's more like what Paul Newman said in *Cool Hand Luke*—'Life's a bunch of nothin.' "

In his personal life, John was faced with the responsibility for working out some delicate relationships. Michelle was getting older, and he needed to create an emotional situation for her that was both comfortable and flexible, regardless of whether she was living at his house or with Cil. He found a great deal of support and understanding from both Vicky and Cil in this matter. With Cil, his relationship was tempered by his awareness that "I wouldn't have been where I was if it hadn't been for her. I'd known her since I was fifteen years old, and I realized that just because your feelings change, you don't just go tell one of your closest friends to get lost. You know, after we separated, we became better friends than ever before."

At home, John was blissfully happy with Vicky, who was soon pregnant. Both had been content to just cohabitate, but with the pregnancy, plans for divorce and marriage had to be made quickly. A settlement was amiably worked: "Neither of them was out to take advantage of the other," observes Tim Elsner. "Cil wasn't the money-grubbing ex-wife type out to screw him, and John really wanted to be equitable and fair." Gary Boebinger concurs. "John handled it amazingly well. To me, his two greatest accomplishments are the fact that he doesn't drink or do drugs—and the way he handled his divorce."

The wedding took place on May 23, 1981, at Richard and Marilyn's house in Seymour, with Michelle in attendance. Cil Mellencamp, who had helped Vicky pick out her wedding dress, shocked a great many of the two hundred or so people who attended the reception simply by showing up. "What a scene it was," recalls Dave Loncao, the ex–MCA promotion man who had stayed close to John over the years. "There was Vicky, six months pregnant, and Cil, and Michelle, and John, getting married in his folks' backyard. When the ceremony was over, the first thing he did was change into a white T-shirt, jeans ripped at the knees, a red windbreaker; he cleared all the older people away and shouted, 'Okay, let's choose up sides!' Only John Mellencamp could have played football on his wedding day . . ."

As John would later say of that two-year period of emotional searching, the

"Only John Mellencamp could have played football on his wedding day . . ." Left to right are Doc, Ken Aronoff, Ferd, Mike Wanchic, Larry Crane, John, and a pregnant Vicky Mellencamp.

gestation of his next album, "A funny thing happened to me on the way to *American Fool*—I grew up." He paused, laughed. "Well, at least I *started* to . . ."

In the months following his wedding, John says, "I had to face it. My heart and soul were still in music. I still found rock and roll as exhilarating as when I was a kid. And the fact was, what the hell else would I have done? Most normal people had gone to college and gotten real jobs—my job was making records!"

With another child on the way, and with the pressure on him to break through in his career, the stakes had risen dramatically. But, he explains, "I reckoned that if I was going to really give it one more shot, I wanted it to be my *best* shot. Then, if I blew it, I'd have nobody to blame but myself. I'd had it with producers telling me how my songs should sound. It was like somebody coming into your house and telling you how to decorate the place."

The brass at Polygram balked at letting John produce his next album, but after much cajoling and the reassurance that John would be working with a pro, Don Gehman, at his side, the company finally agreed. Everything, from arrangement to final mix, would be John's doing. He recalled his final live appearance of 1980, on the *Tom Snyder Show,* when he had performed "Ain't Even Done with the Night" exactly as he had written it—as a rock song, plain and simple, with sharp teeth and plenty of balls. "I felt loose and comfortable on television for the first time," he says. "I think, at that moment, I took charge, although I might not have realized it. I decided I wanted the next record to be exactly like *that.*"

The songs themselves would be pared down to the barest essentials, each one an exercise in the most spontaneous kind of songwriting. Once he had labored over his songs, dickering endlessly and painfully with images and ideas until the original feeling had been frittered away; but now he'd just sit down and dash them off in minutes, keeping those he liked and chucking the rest in the wastebasket. The band had coalesced by that time into tight fraternity. With his jazz/classical background, Ken Aronoff had evolved into a drummer capable of both power and subtlety—by literally unlearning his technical training, he became a purely intuitive rock musician. Guitarists Mike Wanchic and Larry Crane had learned to complement each other's strengths and weaknesses, forming a potent metal blend of Crane's galloping rhythm style and Wanchic's spare lead work. Within the triad of these three musicians, John began to realize that he might locate the special sound he wanted to achieve on the next record. "It *had* to be different—I wanted people to hear the music coming out of car radios and stop dead in their tracks. I wanted it to sound like the Pittsburgh Steelers on a power sweep, like fifty thousand stomping fans in the bleachers, like the assembly line of a steel mill, like a fucking war; like every rock song I'd ever heard or dreamed about in my life . . ."

These were the feverish hopes and dreams that kept him up nights, lying awake in bed next to his pregnant wife, chain-smoking Marlboros—agonizing over whether the songs were good enough; how the radio people, the record company, the critics would take them. Should he write more? What if he went over budget? He carried these worries just about everywhere he went, except when he would get on his Harley to clear his head in one gut-wrenching, mind-boggling burst of speed along the highway. During those moments, he relished the acuity of consciousness that came from the thrill and the danger of pushing it to the absolute limit; he would see nothing but the gradations of the road, feel nothing but the sharpness of mind and body, the flow of the machine. John had always used motorcycles as his emotional release, as his main form of recreation, but now his riding took on a reckless abandon. One night in early June after a rehearsal, he hopped on his chopper and, just as he was winding it out, at ninety miles per hour, an airedale suddenly appeared in his way. "He passed us on the bike and the dog came out of nowhere," remembers Ken Aronoff. "It was like, 'Oh, there goes our careers!' All you could see were sparks from the bike shooting down the highway." The dog was killed; what saved John's life—as usual, he wasn't wearing a helmet—was his ability to stay with the machine as it went down, then kick free. He was hospitalized with a deep hole in his knee the size of a silver dollar. He was out in two days; by the time he left for Miami's Criteria Studios to begin the record, which would consume the next year and present the greatest challenge of his life, he was hobbling on crutches.

The plan was for John to return from Miami when Vicky went into labor, spend a week, then return to the record. But one night, she was suddenly wracked with labor pains. "Do you want me to come home?" he asked her anxiously over the phone. "No," she told him. "It's probably a false alarm." When the pains got worse, she had to go to the doctor. "You're in labor," he informed her. "But I'm not due for a month and a half! This can't be happening . . ."

John had tried to hold constant reservations on different airlines, but when the big event went down, he couldn't get a flight out. His ex-wife ended up accompanying Vicky into the delivery room. The baby girl entered the world at one o'clock in the morning on July 1, 1981. When John finally arrived, he was even more dazed than he had been after the birth of his first child ("I was too young then to know better!"). Teddi Jo Mellencamp had her mother's blond locks and John's pug nose and insouciant pout. Yes, she had that Bad Mellencamp Family Attitude, too. "The first time I saw her she was in an incubator, but she had this look on her face like, 'What are *you* lookin' at? Why are you standin' around looking at me?' I said, 'Boy, she's butch, isn't she?' "

After a week in Bloomington, John took his wife and child back to Miami and work began in earnest on the record. He had written at least thirty songs, but many had no arrangements. Operating in a do-or-die atmosphere, the band began slowly groping toward the special kind of sound John wanted. Don Gehman, a veteran of productions with Steve Stills, McGuinn Clarke and Hillman, Chicago, and the Bee Gees/Streisand *Guilty* project, quickly ascertained that his ideal role as coproducer on this album would be that of a guide for John, a sort of lightning rod to absorb tensions and deflect the technical problems from the band. Still, even with Gehman's easygoing nature and openminded attitude, the sessions were like pulling teeth. The challenge was

to maximize the band's most natural strong points. "Because the group had developed in the musical isolation of Bloomington," Ken Aronoff explains, "we'd been more or less *forced* to come up with our own style. It had been right in front of our faces and we hadn't realized it." John and Don now had to shepherd this style—a lean, straightahead, classic American power rock—into a simple yet monumental sound. With Gehman's background as an engineer—he had originally designed the rooms at Criteria—he turned out to be the perfect partner in the experiment.

After nine weeks of nonstop work, the band was suffering from advanced burnout, but John had only five or six songs that he considered even halfway up to snuff—only half an album. The mood turned grim and tempers flared. By the end of the sessions, John had fired Doc Rosser and Ferd, who, in a fit

John, Mike Wanchic, and co-producer Don Gehman.

(Neil Zlozower)

of pique, had ripped off his bass guitar and smashed it to smithereens on the studio floor. In truth, losing Rosser turned out to be a blessing in disguise: John's music had always been unnecessarily piano based; now, without Doc, he was forced to work with only the most organic ingredients of his band.

The songs that finally made it on to the LP included "Hand to Hold Onto," an anthem to the simple human need for companionship and love. The sentiment of the song might not have been terribly original, but it came straight from John's heart, and the music revealed the band at its best—the guitars juxtaposed perfectly, the singing pure emotion, the energy controlled yet jubilant.

"Thundering Hearts," a furious, hard-kicking rocker with slashing guitars, epitomized the developing direction of *American Fool*. The entire song is built around Aronoff's drumming, for which a very special recording technique was evolving. With Aronoff's kit now tuned to perfection and close-miked, the large room of the studio was, in essence, turned into one huge drum booth; the drums were recorded and mixed through individual microphones, as well as through an ambient room mike that picked them up with the rest of the band. It was a painstaking process, but the effects were explosive, like a shattering barrage of artillery.

Among the other Miami songs ("Weakest Moments," "Close Enough for Rock & Roll," "Cats in the Kitchen") was "Jack and Diane," a perplexing "little ditty" that nobody knew quite what to do with. The music was a producer's nightmare—a patchwork-quilt of acoustic chords and notes slapped up against power rock chords, piano, basslines, drumrolls, hand claps, and choruses—all of it collected on two reels of two-inch tape. The lyrics derived from the pervasive sense of nostalgia that John had been feeling about his youth—"In fact, just the other day I was telling Larry Crane I was thinking about writing a song saying I'd trade everything I've got right now for one night of youth again," he related to Zach Dunkin of the *Indianapolis Times* in December 1979. The song was a portrait of a boy and girl growing up in the Heartland. More than anything else, "Jack and Diane" is John Cougar's attestation to novelist Gabriel Garcia Marquez's adage that every writer spends the rest of his life writing about his youth. The lyrics represent a decoction of his own life and times, but also the life of every kid who grows up in small town USA. Snippets and images came together in collage fashion, like the chilli dogs at the Tastee Freez that they suck on (there was never a Tastee Freez in Seymour, only in Bloomington). Jack was going to be a "football star," Diane a "debutante in the back of Jacky's car." When Jacky gets the high-falutin' notion, "I think we ought to run off to the city," Diane has the simple, folksy wisdom to tell him they're better off where they are—"Baby, we ain't missin' a thing."

Underneath the lives of the characters is the songwriter's bittersweet sense of growing older, more jaded and deadened by the onslaught of life, by its mundane moments: "Ooooh, yeah, life goes on, long after the thrill of living is gone." "Hold onto sixteen as long as you can," he exhorts the kids. "Changes come around real soon make us women and men." And there it was.

For a while John thought seriously about scrapping the song. The words seemed too banal, and the band had reached an impasse of energy and creativity. Finally, the band and his wife talked him into keeping it, and then he scrubbed all further recording sessions and sent everybody home. He was convinced that he was blowing his last shot. Had you told him that the reels with "Jack and Diane" contained the rough parts of a classic American pop song, he would have laughed in your face.

The fall months passed dismally in Bloomington—the album was already grossly over budget, and the delivery date had been bumped back. Some of the Miami songs were useable; others needed more work. The big problem was that the album lacked what John considered to be a standout song for a leadoff hit single—an essential requirement if the album was ever to break through. "We started playing together, just working stuff out," Ken Aronoff recalls, "and that's when things all of a sudden started to jell. We realized what kind of band we really were. That's when 'Hurts So Good' came up."

The song that would finally put John Cougar on the map was born on a fall afternoon when his old friend George Green, who worked answering phones for him while he was away, half-jokingly suggested to John that they write a song about something that "hurts so good." Green and John had collaborated on lyrics as kids in Seymour and lately had put their heads together for "Thundering Hearts." "We were laughing about it," Green recalls. "You know, thinking about the kind of things that hurt so good—like scratching a case of athlete's foot." John went upstairs; the verses came to him in the shower and he wrote the words in soap on the shower wall. "He called me up the next day and said, 'Come on over and hear the song,'" Green says. "We sat and worked on it . . ." The lyrics, a strutting bit of libidinous oats-feeling, contained a reference to a longing for "those young boy days," with images like "Sink your teeth into my bones"; the chorus turned on "Sometimes love don't feel like it should/You know it hurts so good."

Round two of *American Fool* took place at Cherokee Studios in Los

Angeles. But now, magically, effortlessly, things started falling into place. The music for "Hurts So Good" evolved in the vein of "Hand to Hold Onto" and "Thundering Hearts," but it was still more basic and more defined. With George "Chocolate" Perry on bass, they cut the song fifty-five times—all live takes. John added a cover version of "China Girl," a stunner by Joe New and Jeff Silbur that Levon Helm had recorded several years earlier. Finally "Jack and Diane" was also constructed, with the help of Mick Ronson, who had been called into the Miami sessions to add some juice when the energy level was flagging. Ronson suggested adding a vocal bridge—"Let it rock, let it roll"—where John had originally put organ, and the elements were slowly, painstakingly blended. "The song was a never-ending battle," says Larry Crane. "It took two twenty-four-track machines—the mixing was like editing *Ben Hur* or something." The production was a masterpiece of careful modulation. "What took so long was getting the song to sound the way it does without putting ten million instruments on it," John explains. "On the record there are rarely more than four instruments playing at once. I was learning that it's so much harder to be simpler." Even though the playback pleased everyone, John was still convinced that the song was a longshot. "I thought *maybe* it would be a good novelty song."

The album was finished after eight months, at a cost of over a quarter of a million dollars. John would name it *American Fool,* after a song he had recorded that did not even make it onto the LP. In an age of conservative, no-risk packaging and mass marketing, it seemed a peculiar, confusing, alienating, self-deprecating title; yet the message and theme of the record is right there: John Cougar was just another guy out there, just another fool like everybody else.

The album would also be released without printed lyrics. "Well, I don't consider myself a writer," John would bluntly tell people. "*Tennessee Williams* was a writer. Personally, I ain't got shit to say."

Listening sessions are a tradition at record companies; an artist under contract comes in with master tapes, and the top executives all sit around together and get their first earful of what they hope will be a big moneymaker. Often these meetings are corporate seances of gushing optimism and congratulation, during which grown men have been known to jump up and down and squeal like teenagers, bruiting about words like *megahit, monster, multiplatinum,* and *potential Grammy* about some of the most mediocre product imaginable. The first playback of John Cougar's new album in Polygram President Chip Taylor's corner office on the thirty-fourth floor of 810 Seventh

Avenue surely made history, then, for one reason alone: Not one of the people packed into the office thought any of the songs had even the slightest chance; moreover, they thought the songs were trash, downright excrement. Staring with disbelief at their long faces, Russel Shaw was thinking, *God, what am I going to tell John?*

As it turned out, John Cougar had already had an inkling about Polygram's negative reaction when Vice President Bob Sherwood had flown down to Miami to listen to tapes. But since the second round of recording and the mixing, John felt confident that the record was the best of his life. At that point, he heard from somebody at CBS Records—"Hey, man, the word's out on the street that Polygram doesn't like your record!"—and that's when he started to worry. When he called Shaw and was informed that the rumor was true, he got on a plane for New York, filled with dread.

At a second playback meeting, John sat there for hours, trying to choke back the anger and the humiliation. *This is a nightmare I'm having,* he kept telling himself. *This isn't really happening . . .*

"There isn't *any*thing on the album like 'I Need a Lover' or 'Ain't Even Done with the Night,' " he was told.

"If I start repeating myself already, I'm *dead*," John countered.

"The album is too rough, too ragged. It's going to *ruin* your career. There's nothing like it even being played on the radio . . ."

"Well," John asked, "what about 'Hurts So Good'?"

"Top Forty, *maybe*."

John Cougar had to face the unpalatable truth: There were powerful men in that room, who controlled his life at that moment, who still thought of him as somebody who was trying to be another Neil Diamond. Worse, Taylor and Sherwood had come up with a plan—adding the Muscle Shoals rhythm section and Memphis horns to the tracks—to salvage the album. That was the last straw—John Cougar had reached that critical juncture where he knew he had to stand fast and not give an inch.

"Look, either you release the record *exactly* the way it is, or don't release it at all—I'll take it somewhere else!"

Perhaps the only person at Polygram who sought to reassure John Cougar was Bill Cataldo, the gruff-talking Peter Falk–lookalike in radio promotion. "I had lunch with John and Russel Shaw at Gallagher's, and John was a fucking nervous wreck," Cataldo recollects. "I told him I thought the album was going to be huge. I loved 'Jack and Diane,' but you couldn't come with that as your first single."

Apparently, Polygram's strategy was to release only one single from the

John and friends boogie-down in "Hurts So Good." The bespectacled gentleman with the moustache directly over John's right shoulder is none other than Mark Ripley.

album—"Hurts So Good"—and hope that if nobody heard how lousy the rest was, it might sell a few copies. Billy Gaff wasn't buying the plan. Gaff recognized that it was time for him to once again intercede personally in Cougar's career, and he had flown in from London at the first sign of trouble. His argument to the Polygram brass was simple and forceful: "Look, even *I* didn't like John's last album, and it sold over a quarter of a million. Let's just release the songs and let the kids decide. Your job isn't to *like* the music, it's to *sell* it."

Reluctantly, Polygram agreed to unleash Bill Cataldo with "Hurts So Good" as the first single, followed by "Jack and Diane" and "Hand to Hold Onto."

The videos for the songs, which were in the can before the album was released, were offered to MTV, the newly established Warner–Amex cable station that would revolutionize the marketing and promotion of records, giving a much-needed shot in the arm to the sagging music industry. All three were low-budget productions, again produced by Simon Fields, an urbane young Englishman who was moving into the new vanguard of music video producers. "Hurts So Good" was conceived as a party piece, much as John saw the record. The video was shot in the tiny town of Medora, where John's cousin and later bodyguard, Tracy Cowles, would open a tavern that would attract wolfpacks of bearded, tattooed, stringy-haired Hoosier bikers. From the beginning, the video was a lark; John invited friends and family from all over Indiana for the shoot, which took over the whole town. He performs the song in the bar, standing on a table next to a slinky brunette in stockings and garters, with chains draped across her chest like bandoleers. On the tattering beat, in closeup, he brings his hand up underneath her happily undulating crotch. The gesture was performed with such endearing, good-natured relish that it makes you laugh with recognition that, yes, *any* red-blooded American boy would grope this lady given a similar chance. The image would eventually get John into trouble, despite its obviously harmless message, and would become the prototype for heavy-metal clichés to follow on MTV—literally hundreds of long-haired, bare-chested performers standing with guitars like Norse gods before the cameras, being solemnly worshipped by girls in lacy lingerie.

"Jack and Diane," on the other hand, depicts John and Vicky as a homespun hero and heroine; the life and times of the protagonists are rendered through the collected photos of Mr. and Mrs. Mellencamp, all of them seen through flashing boxes of the past and present (at one point, John even has Vicky on his lap, with "his hands between her knees"—just like old Jack.) The present-day footage was shot with eight-millimeter film to give it a home-movie quality, and it was personally edited by Simon Fields. "Hand to Hold Onto," undoubtedly the most mundane of the three videos, is a rather straightahead treatment of the band performing perched over the Bloomington quarry.

With the videos ready to go and the record nearing release, the only thing that still remained uncertain was a high-profile launching for the album.

As Billy Gaff's partner in Riva, Rod Stewart had always insisted that Gaff never evoke Stewart's illustrious name to try to further the slow-moving career of John Cougar. Russel Shaw had always considered the stipulation unreasonable and even mean-spirited, but he had respected it until he tried to get John Cougar on *Saturday Night Live*. Russel was passionate about the

(Neil Zlozower)

"He started blowing people away on that tour . . ." Larry, John, and new bass player Toby Myers.

American Fool and also about John and Vicky. He knew that an appearance as the musical guest on the highly rated show, always watched closely by radio and record retail people, might easily decide whether or not "Hurts So Good" was added to playlists all over America. When the show's programmers steadfastly refused John Cougar, Russel went straight to producer Dick Ebersol. "Look, we did right by you with Rod when you wanted him for the show," Russel said. "Do us this favor." He continued to harangue and plead; Ebersol finally agreed.

American Fool was released, appropriately, on April Fool's Day, 1982. That same day, John debuted "Hurts So Good" on Kid Leo's show at WMMS in Cleveland. "The first time I heard it, I knew it would take him to platinum status," Leo recalls. "The effect was pretty amazing—it became an immediate high-request number." Of course, Cleveland had always been one of John Cougar's strongest markets; the real test would come elsewhere.

A week later, John appeared on *Saturday Night Live,* after two straight weeks of night and day rehearsals with a new bass player named Toby Myers. Myers was a good-looking, gangly fellow who had recorded a few records with a band called Pure Funk and had then spent years as a member of Roadmaster, one of Indiana's most popular club bands. He had never played a large concert venue, let alone national television; fortunately, he was so excited by the opportunity that his exhilaration exceeded his terror. "John was nervous about wanting to do really well," Myers says. "The sound checks were really tense—you could have cut the tension with a knife. Of course, now I can't even watch the tapes of the performance because I was so happy just to *be* there that I was beaming like an idiot through the whole thing . . ."

The performance resonated with John's freeform energy and confidence—for the first time in his life, he appeared truly comfortable with himself on television. Dressed in a pair of black-leather motorcycle pants, he roamed the NBC stage like a wild beast in search of prey. Both songs, "Hurts So Good" and a version of "Ain't Even Done with the Night," done *American Fool*-style, popped off perfectly; even a dissonant guitar note sounded right. The experience of the moment was beyond any review, beyond chart positions or sales figures. "Everything changed," John says. "We realized we weren't the greatest band, but didn't *have* to be. The feeling we had was that we were just going to do what we wanted to and not worry anymore. I was just going to write songs and produce the records, and if it didn't sell, so what? The important thing was that we wouldn't have to take any more shit."

The style of the music, as rudimentary as it was, was markedly different

(Neil Zlozower)

from anything on the radio at the time. During that first week after the show, Bill Hard picked "Hurts So Good" to fly and committed himself in his tipsheet. "You knew you could count on everybody to play it," he says. "It had pop appeal, rock appeal—all kinds of crossover possibilities."

Just as a boxer needs to have all the basic punches in his repertoire—jab, hook, uppercut, knock-out haymaker—to be truly competitive in the ring, an artist needs the combination of a good song on the charts and an extensive, high-drawing tour to translate regional appeal or cult status into national popularity. With 110 dates booked as the opening act for Heart and "Hurts So Good" cutting up the charts, John Cougar possessed these tools for the first time in his career.

Traveling in a rented King Air six-seat turbo-plane, with Ted Mellencamp road managing and Russel Shaw in constant attendance, John felt more like he could concentrate on the quality of his performances, which seemed to get more physical with each night. "He started blowing people away on that tour," recalls Dave Loncao, the promotion man and friend who had seen him bomb in Cincinnati on his very first tour. "That's when you could really see it all coming together for him up there. Before that tour, there was always good stuff and stuff that didn't quite work—a song, a movement, an off-the-cuff remark that either went over great or fell flat. Now there were no flat notes in the performance."

The pace of the tour was grueling. To remember where he was, as the dates started blurring together, John had to tape the city they were playing to the back of his guitar. As the summer progressed and "Hurts So Good" continued to climb, the responses of the audience became steadily louder, crazier. In San Francisco, when he performed his nightly feat of leaping wildly into the audience, he almost didn't survive: Girls surrounded him like wildcats, ripping off his shirt, pulling out a hank of his hair. "In Orange County, we had to stop the show and make an announcement for the girls to stop jumping on the stage," John recalls with utter amazement. "I'd played there before, but they'd never done that! I felt, Who *am* I, Rick Springfield or somebody?"

The show now featured a ringing cover of the Stones' "Can't Always Get What You Want," a kicked-out version propelled into high voltage by the guitars of Larry Crane and Mike Wanchic and by the backup singing of Pat Peterson, a soul belter who now provided the vocal pyrotechnics behind "Thundering Hearts." "His show was hardly the last word in slick showmanship," noted Mark Rowland in *Musician* later that year, "yet Cougar remains such an ingratiating presence that all the raw edges worked in his favor." Observing that "even the band's artless stage presence" helped "eradicate

(Neil Zlozower)

With favorite back-up singer, Pat Peterson.

the barriers between fans and performers," Rowland likened the show to becoming "privy to a giant, boisterous rent party. And in the true spirit of adolescent excess," he wrote, "Cougar not only tried to leap into the audience, but for the final reprise of 'Hurts So Good,' went one better by hoisting the front row teenies onto the stage. There, he and thirty of Denver's cutest cavorted arm in arm like some flashback to a beer blast, while the rest of the band nonchalantly kicked out the jams and the security goons looked on in glazed bewilderment."

With "Hurts So Good" at No. 10, with a bullet, Bill Cataldo decided to release "Jack and Diane." The strategy was a gamble: Usually record companies wait until one song reaches its zenith on the chart before dropping another single from an album. "All my instincts told me that 'Hurts So Good' would keep traveling up," Cataldo says. "My plan was to drop 'Jack and Diane' and catch two singles in the Top Ten at the same time. If it works, you look like a genius; if it doesn't, you look like an asshole."

The response from radio was overwhelming: "Jack and Diane" showed quick strength in AOR, whereas "Hurts So Good" had been immediately strong in the Top Forty format. It was a record company's dream: two singles working both radio markets simultaneously and crossing over into the other markets at the same time. According to Bill Hard, "Jack and Diane" became "one of the ultimate" radio songs because it tapped directly into the motherlode of Middle America. "It had one of the slowest reduction rates in terms of how much it was coming through the music lists," Hard points out. "It was really the first Cougar song to totally dominate on the telephone—people apparently couldn't get enough of it. Again and again, it topped the most-requested-song lists."

But the potential of two simultaneous hit singles was almost completely lost on John Cougar, who was now swept into the surreal, nocturnal life of the tour. The exhilaration of his performances became greater as the nights wore on, a deep release of emotional and physical energies that was contradicted by a hundred little tensions—the constant waiting, the tedium of hotel rooms and endless hamburgers-to-go, the stultifying routine of moving from plane to car to hotel to concert to plane. "John gets bored easily on the road," Ted Mellencamp points out. "He likes all the creature comforts he can get, and he's always looking for a way to amuse himself." Consequently, the tour did not lack that particular brand of impish Mellencamp antics, most of them directed against Rus Shaw, who was so jaded by the life-style of big-time rock & roll touring that he would oftentimes go straight from the hotel to the plane in his bathrobe. "I was thrown nude into a concert hall," Shaw admits with comical nonchalance. "I'm a kid at heart, and I can take those practical jokes." And, as usual, "by the end of the tour, Ted and I had already had one of our fights," John laughs.

Far more dangerous and upsetting was the time John and his entire family were almost wiped out while flying into Lexington, Kentucky, on the King Air. John had accepted a random date as a headliner on one of his off days, and his plane was approaching the small airport, with his wife and two daughters aboard, when a drastic windshift caused it to overshoot the runway.

Caught helplessly in the powerful current, the plane flipped over completely and went veering off for another approach. "I thought it was all over," John says. "I blew my lunch all over the cabin!" After a few nasty words with the pilot, he arrived at the concert hall, shaken and ill, only to become unnerved by the badly mixed sound. The ensuing explosion—a vintage bit of Mellencamp temper—was witnessed by opening act Huey Lewis, sitting out in the darkened house, who had no idea of what John Cougar had just been through. "Wow, he tied into those production guys like you wouldn't believe," Lewis relates. "He was screaming over the microphone. They were completely withered—I felt sorry for them. I just sat there in complete amazement, wondering, 'Who *is* this guy?' "

Nobody but Huey and a few roadies had witnessed that outburst, but in the case of the infamous equipment incident in London, Ontario, on August 30, no less than fourteen thousand people were privy to the spectacle of the old Bad Mellencamp Family Attitude erupting like Mount St. Helens. John was playing nearby in Toronto when promoters called to ask him to join a double bill of Del Shannon and the Beach Boys at an outdoor venue. The band's equipment was packed up with Heart's and couldn't be extricated under the circumstances, but the promoters agreed to provide rental equipment. The

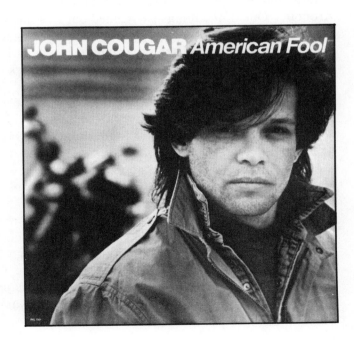

problem began when John and the band arrived to discover that nothing that they'd asked for was there. As John later explained to *Creem,* "Then I find out that before I got on the bill, they'd only sold two thousand tickets. I get added and ten thousand seats are sold out. But the real dastardly deed came when they told my brother Ted . . . that we had to cut our set from fifty-five minutes to thirty-five, because they were running late. I thought the people who paid ten bucks to see this mess are going to get bummed out when the act they paid for only plays thirty-five minutes. They're going to hold it against me, and I ain't got nothing to do with it!"

As soon as the band got onstage and Mike Wanchic hit a chord on his guitar, the rented amp broke; things deteriorated from there. The PA system was inadequate, the microphone a joke. John only got angrier as the minutes passed. He asked the crowd, "How many of you people came to see *us?*" And when the place exploded, he figured that at least he'd let everybody know how he was feeling. What followed was a stinging denunciation of the promoters for "ripping off the kids" by making John and his band play a shortened set on "Tinkertoy" equipment. Promoter Don Jones, waiting offstage, was furious; then, to add insult to injury, John took all the equipment that had failed to meet his expectations and passed it out to the audience: "Here, take this shit—because that's all it is!" "It was funny," offers Kenny Aronoff. "One of the things we handed out was the bass drum. It was quite a sight to see this big drum being passed over their heads—it looked like it was walking away by itself! Then I realized that my favorite drum pedal, which I'd brought myself, had also walked! 'Hey, give me back that thing!' I tried to get a roadie to go after it, but he was pertrified."

John flounced offstage to encounter Jones and several of the Beach Boys, who reportedly had wanted to pull the plug on his little tirade, scowling angrily. "Why don't one of you motherfuckers just *say* something to me about it!"

Just then he felt a tap on his shoulder. "Nice show, Jerry Lee!" exclaimed his cousin, Tracy Cowles. Fortunately, the humor of the comment disabused him of the notion to clock the promoter in the eye.

"We hightailed it out of that town pretty quick," recalls Larry Crane. "We were afraid we were going to be stuck at the airport and lynched or something, so we had to get special clearance to fly out that night!"

The incident was widely reported on the wire services, but promoter Jones's version was the one quoted: "The guy snapped," he said of John, claiming that several girls in the audience had been hurt by cymbals irresponsibly flung into the crowd like lethal Frisbees.

"Nobody got hurt at all," counters John, "otherwise I would have been sued, believe me. I wasn't sorry for what I did because they had no right to take advantage of the kids like that, but I felt bad about the situation, so I promised to come back and play for the people of London—but this time with my own equipment—at my own expense."

Controversy seemed to stick like flypaper to John Cougar wherever he went on the *American Fool* tour, and such incidents only seemed to reinforce the prevailing view in the press that he was indeed some loud-mouthed, punk kid from the Midwest who had gotten lucky with a song on the radio. For his own part, John told an interviewer, "I think that for all of these temper tantrum things that I've been accused of, if you really evaluate the situation, you'll agree that I was right and I was being exploited. You'll always have your skeptics, right? I've read a lot about how, 'He's a baby, he has to have everything his way and he's cocky and arrogant.' But when it comes right down to it, I have to make my own decisions. I mean, nobody says that Bobby Knight is a nice guy, right? There are times you have to say, 'Well, this is the way it is and this is what I'm going to do.' "

Despite its meteoric ascent up the charts, *American Fool* was meeting with a strong critical backlash. The LP cover displays a peevish-looking Cougar photographed by Jurgen Vollmer. John is wearing his oldest Army jacket, with plenty of stubble on his face and a squinty, cynical frown that seems to anticipate the public relations problems he would face after the release of the

LP. *All right,* the cover conveys, *I know you guys are gonna take a swipe at me, so you might as well get it over with . . .*

"He was *very* sensitive to his press," remarks Polygram publicist Sherry Ring Ginsberg. "From the very beginning he said to me, 'I do not want you taking out the bad reviews. I want to see the bad along with the good.' It made sense when I realized how much music mattered to him. He'd always ask me why I thought somebody wrote such and such a thing. See, he respected a lot of the critics because he'd always read them himself over the years."

Sherry Ring Ginsberg's own preconceptions about John Cougar mirrored what would become the larger problems of his press relations. "I'd been actually *scared* of him before I first met him," she admits, "because so many people had warned me, 'Oh, be careful of John, watch what you say—don't go near him!' I was really nervous. Then when I got to really know him, I realized that nobody knew who he really was. What we had to do was just tell people the John Cougar story and let them develop their own opinions."

On *American Fool,* particularly, the spectre of Bruce Springsteen (and Bob Seger) continued to haunt John Cougar. What chagrined John was his certainty that the album was so far removed from Springsteen in sound and style that the comparisons would finally come to an end. *Rolling Stone,* in a review by Ken Emerson, led the way: "John 'Cougar' Mellencamp can't help it. All he has to do is open his mouth and out oozes insincerity, the snake oil of patent imitations of Bruce Springsteen and Bob Seger. Or for good measure, he'll pour on a little Tom Petty or Graham Parker. It's not just Cougar's hoarse, choked tenor that sounds overfamiliar; his secondhand serenades to teenage titillation at the car wash and the Tastee-Freez have also been heard elsewhere."

Bob Christgau, one of the deans of rock criticism, gave the record a "B" in his Consumer Guide column in the *Village Voice:* "The breakthrough fluke of the year has it all over his predecessors in REO Speedwagon—Bob Seger, Cougar's current role model, has been dreaming of riffs with this much melodic crunch since *Night Moves,* and when I don't think about the whys and the wherefores they satisfy my mainstream cravings. But the guy is a phony on the face of it, and not in a fun way—anybody with the gall to tell teen America that once you pass 16 'the thrill of living is gone' has been slogging toward stardom for so long that he never noticed what happened to Shaun Cassidy."

Dave Marsh, a longtime champion of both Springsteen and Seger, in a syndicated review, also dimissed the record: "Listen, I'm the biggest Bruce Springsteen fan in the world—or near enough—and these croaked-voice

"As the summer progressed and "Hurts So Good" continued to climb, the responses of the audience became steadily louder, crazier . . ."

Bossisms don't even begin to woo me, so how hopeless Cougar's hard-guy post must really be, it's hard to imagine. Despite Cougar's boast, not close enough for rock and roll—or anything else except cynical marketability."

Other critics didn't even want to hear the record to begin with, but perhaps the most insufferable slings came from people who wouldn't even give him credit for having songs on the charts. According to Jonathan Takiff of the *Philadelphia Daily News,* his success had nothing to do with the songs; it was "all in the timing." Neither Springsteen nor Seger had albums out at the time, explained Takiff in his column, and Springsteen had issued *Nebraska,* his gloomy, acoustic album "that totally rejected his romantic image," and had to alienate many of his less committed fans. This opened the doors even further for Cougar to waltz in with "elementary grade Springsteen numbers" like "Hurts So Good" and "Jack and Diane."

Needless to say, these pronouncements were difficult to swallow. In retrospect, one has to wonder what on earth "Hurts So Good" had to do with Springsteen or Seger to begin with (vocal similarities aside). Granted, the essential message of "Hand to Hold Onto" was related to Springsteen's "Hungry Heart," and the teen turf of "Jack and Diane" might have been a distant cousin to Seger's "Night Moves," but sooner or later all rock & roll writers utilize these themes (Bruce's "Glory Days" is a perfect example). In John's case, the theme was filtered through his own developing musical sensibility, reaching an individual sound and expression—the style was drastically different from anything being played on the radio at the time—and therein lies the rub: It wasn't so much the music that the critics found objectionable, but John Cougar himself. Critics who had made a life's avocation out of insisting that rock was something much more than merely a good time or big business—indeed, that the best rock aspired to consciousness-awakening, to being at the cutting edge of social change—were obviously not going to be impressed by the lyrics of "Hurts So Good." The irony of the situation was that a part of John Cougar agreed with them, which is precisely why he went out of his way to downplay the significance of his own songs, even as they rocketed up the charts—he was being honest about his work. Nevertheless, he strongly felt that he deserved better. "Sometimes I don't feel like I need all the derogatory slams," he said in one interview, "because I'm not that bad a guy. I mean, there are times I have trouble liking myself like anybody else . . ."

On the other hand, there was always a part of John Cougar that liked a good scuffle (indeed, thrived on it) and that enjoyed thumbing his nose at the people who didn't like him. "I have an image problem," he later admitted to

Musician's Mark Rowland. "But the thing I'm most proud of, in spite of everything, is that I'm still popular despite all the fashions, all the trends and all the critical bullshit. I'm still popular, and that's what's great. It's almost like high school—the idea of, 'I'm not playing by your rules, and if you don't like it, kiss my ass. Okay?' "

In truth, John Cougar appreciated music as the most personal of things, recognizing that all of us—artist, fan, critic, industry people—are captives of the most boiling prejudices. "When you listen to a record," he says, "you can have a good set of ears on or a bad set of ears before you even hear it. It's all in the perception . . ." These biases, pro and con, are what subject pop music to the same forces of supply and demand that regulate any free market economy—assuming, of course, that the product even makes it to the market place. Having the critics on your side certainly makes life easier and can be instrumental in popularizing unknown artists. The critical establishment exerts an undeniable influence within the industry itself, but, in the end, what is written in *Rolling Stone* or the *New York Times* has very little to do with how the vast majority of people feel about music, with what gets played on the radio or whether or not the consumer plunks down money for a cassette tape of *American Fool*. However, in John Cougar's case, the bad reviews were a matter of pride that had a direct bearing on his self-image. He could accept being called tasteless, an abject failure; but to be accused of insincerity, of ripping off other people's attitudes and turning them into bad clichés, was something else. Thus, even before *American Fool* had peaked, he saw his next big hurtle—being taken seriously by the critics—form on the horizon.

Meanwhile, publicist Howard Bloom was hired onto the record to counteract the negative press and promote the positive. Thin, wiry, always favoring his aviator's glasses and leather jacket, Bloom had consolidated a reputation as one of the industry's best-known press agents, whose clients ranged from superstars, who hired him to keep the press off their backs, to relatively unknown acts, who required intricate, step-by-step campaigns of media infiltration and saturation. With a mind that combined the expansiveness of a philosopher with the cold, analytical qualities of a statistician, he was certainly not the average public-relations mouthpiece.

As Bloom saw it, his assignment was "to show people that there is a *human being* there and not some corny pastiche—really a person with strong roots and feelings, somebody with a consistent point of view that comes from his experience." To discover that person for himself, Bloom flew to Indiana to meet John and found him grilling hamburgers with Mark Ripley out on his driveway. He rode dirt bikes with him and talked with him about his life. "I'd noticed the tremendous sense of nostalgia in the songs," Bloom relates, "and I just asked him what was so great about being sixteen, and for the next six straight hours he went on about his youth. What unfolded was a veritable *Spoon River Anthology,* with peculiar characters the likes of which I'd never encountered. I was staggered; by the time he was finished, I realized that not only was this person a true product of the American Heartland, but that the Heartland was, as Sherwood Anderson had said, 'the land of the grotesques.' "

Bloom found what he called a "PR person's dream" in John Cougar. He sees public relations largely as a function of "instant myth-making." "The best PR campaigns are the ones that make use of the myths that capture something about Americans," he explains, "about how they see themselves and what they want to be—it's finding that value and joining it with twenty million people who need it." Bloom had located one of these basic American values in Cougar and, in doing so, had found a PR handle. "Integrity is central to John Cougar," he observes. "The attitude that I found was, 'I don't care what you say, I'm worth something.' He was basically saying, 'I'm just a fool, just a nobody, and I don't pretend to *be* anybody—but nobodies are *important,* and don't ever try to put us down!' He was ready to defy every conceivable authority just to be able to say, 'Don't try to tell me how to run my life.' That's a substantial contribution to people in a world where they always have to compromise themselves just to scratch out a living."

Bloom now tried to craft this populist appeal into an image and to parlay it into good press. But what finally started putting John Cougar across to the media was nothing more than the attraction of his infectious personality. He went after the press exactly as he had gone after his audiences, seducing them with his honesty, his ingenuous charm, his humor. When it became apparent that *American Fool* was no mere fluke but a phenomenon, the press started asking him what had finally made the difference: "To be honest," he told the *Cincinnati Post,* "I just think I've been around so long that they done used up everybody else!" When interviewed on NBC's *Live at Five* in New York, he insisted on playing with Jack Cafferty's teleprompter before the interview went ahead. When *Rolling Stone* sent Andrew Slater out to do a short piece, John and Bo picked him up at the Bloomington airport on their Harleys, without helmets: "Hope you don't mind riding with Bo," John said. "He's really a safe rider. Hasn't had a wreck in weeks. Honest!" When Polygram threw a birthday party for him after he played the Meadowlands, he celebrated by dunking the diminutive Sherry Ring Ginsberg into the four-foot cake. "All the writers were taken with him," she recalls. "I kept hearing things like, 'He's just like my best friend!' They were beginning to see that John was very down to earth, funny, very forthright, and especially, very talkative. On the other hand, sometimes he'd say *too* much and put his foot right in his mouth."

The experience of *Rolling Stone* associate editor Chris Connelly typifies the thawing attitude of the press toward John Cougar. "I listened to his records and was surprised at how good they were compared to what I was expecting," says Connelly. "I didn't know anything about him as a person. He was still out opening for Heart and really waxing their tails, and yet he was very gracious about the situation, which might have been awkward. He said the kind of things onstage that I would have liked to hear as a member of the audience: 'If you see me on the street, just stop me and tell me, "Hey, John, we saw you in Hays, Kansas.' "

What Connelly found, to his surprise, was not only a good story for his magazine, but a person who became a close friend. "He was really open about things," he says, "to a degree that was very unusual in this business. I was impressed by how voluble he was and how eager to talk—particularly how much he knew about music and how much he *cared* about it. I was really touched by his friendship, by his keeping in touch and his desire to know what *I* thought about things. He had a real willingness to share the things in his life that were not a part of my own experience."

What emerged from Connelly's interviews was the first balanced portrait of John Cougar, filled with revealing anecdotes, humor—at one point John compared songwriting to "getting a hard-on—I just don't wanna think about it"—and perceptions about Cougar's many paradoxes. Connelly wrote: "Cougar's battle for individuality isn't a battle to impose his thinking on anyone, it's a fight to get out from under all the philosophies that everyone— from his family to the record industry to music critics—have imposed on him. Rather than offering himself up as a storyteller from the neglected Midwest, Cougar is adamant that his music is meaningless. His songs are 'real insignificant bullshit.' He hates being taken seriously. And he goes far beyond that: Politics is bullshit. Life is boring, but, hey, you can deal with it. But this nihilistic attitude doesn't do him any good, either. It occurs to me that this googly-eyed, gabby, good-hearted little guy is still hanging on a cross. Only this time, it's a cross he made himself."

Likewise, *Musician*'s Mark Rowland was getting a new fix on the inconsistencies that made John Cougar tick: "Consider: an alienated and aimless product of small-town Indiana—who spent seven arduous years proving himself as a songwriter and musician. . . . who got into the music biz by letting

With Sherry Ring Ginsberg, after plopping her onto his birthday cake.

David Bowie's manager completely make over his image, even changing his name. A relaxed, happy-go-lucky personality—who enjoys playing the brat with almost fiendish glee . . .''

Little by little, more of the real John Cougar emerged in these stories, but the transition was by no means totally smooth or without tumult. Before these articles went to press, the writers had already witnessed the debacle of his appearance on CBS's *Nightwatch,* along with about one million other viewers. The incident (hereinafter called *Cougar* vs. *Jeter*) is worth delving into. Apart from its pure entertainment value, it represents a graphic display of his most basic attitudes under fire, and constitutes the most public trotting out of the old Bad Mellencamp Family Attitude in the annals of Mellencam-panna . . .

Originally John did not want to appear on the show, but had been persuaded by Bloom, Ring Ginsberg, Russel Shaw, and others that the program offered a media "coming out" of sorts. John continued to resist—the idea of being on a talk show made him frankly squeamish—but when one of the producers actually came to his hotel room with the sly argument that John should do the show "so that other music people would get credibility," he had said, "Uh-huh." When he appeared at the studio where the newfangled late-night talkathon taped, accompanied by Vicky and Howard Bloom, he encountered a teleprompter that read *John Cougar: The Cat of Rock and Roll.* ("I saw that intro and thought to myself, 'Oh, no, who *writes* this copy anyway?' " he recalled.) He also met Felicia Jeter for the first time: a handsome black woman in her thirties, poised, aggressive, and sassy.

The first segment went well, with Felicia wishing John a happy thirty-first birthday. After the station break, she introduced the video for "Hurts So Good," but not before John said, "Maybe I should preface this by saying that this tape is tongue-in-cheek. I get a lot of people who think this is *serious.''* The clip rolled. Of course, they aired the raciest part of the promo, with John up on the table with the woman in fishnets and chains, complete with the little crotch grope. The cut back to the studio revealed Felicia coiled up in her chair like a snake about to strike. *"Chains,''* she observed, a frown spread across her face, "and *leather?''*

The confrontation developed fast: Cougar tried to slither away with a few jocular remarks, but Felicia came after him like a shark after bloody meat. "Now, wait a minute," she said, a bit like a parent admonishing a child after throwing up dinner, "how are you gonna tell your *eleven-year-old daughter* about this film clip here?"

John began by saying, "Well, I mean, she sits, she watches, and she thinks this is what rock and roll is all about."

"*Is* it?"

"Yeah, more or less. Rock and roll, you know—'Bebopalula' to me was sexual, violent—that's what the Who were about, that's what the Rolling Stones were about . . ."

Felicia's retort was like a well-aimed arrow: "Now that *you're* an adult, you're in charge. Is *that* what you want out there?"

To John Mellencamp, the notion that he was "in charge," that he had become "the establishment," was tantamount to insanity. He laughed and said, "Bull . . ."

But Jeter begged to differ. With the most condescending of smiles, she announced, "You're the grown people now."

Before the segment was over John had used the word *crap*—it rolled rather awkwardly off his tongue on national television—about the stuff that he had been made to watch as a kid. Then he went on to call the American Dream a myth: the college degree, the good job, marriage to the girl next door—"It doesn't work like *that,*" he said contemptuously. As the segment trailed away into the station break, John was hoping that Felicia would break the clench and move on to another subject. Instead, she came back and threw him a left hook: "John, you once said something about John Wayne, something about his having left a *scar* on the American public . . . What was that about?"

It was one of those typically colorful Mellencampian utterances that journalists always seemed to seize and feature prominently in their stories, with troublesome results—like the time he called Gary, Indiana, "the asshole of America." It was just the way he expressed himself—injudicious, yes, but to many an undeniable part of his appeal and charm. Once he had told this writer, on the record, that one of his greatest ambitions was to grow old and become a "fat, obnoxious prick" like Marlon Brando. Of course, this was John's way of saying that he really *respected* Brando—that he aspired to become, like Brando in his golden years, an overweight, difficult curmudgeon who could say and do whatever he pleased. Now he sighed and answered Jeter's question by patiently explaining that the macho culture exemplified by Wayne had taken its toll on men and on the relationship between the sexes. For someone so often accused of being macho himself, it was an honest response that revealed how his attitudes had evolved. Again Jeter went after him: "Is this the same guy talking to me that just told me *whips* and *chains* and all that stuff is okay to show your eleven-year-old daughter?"

From this point on, communication deteriorated and the two parties hurtled inexorably toward war.

JOHN: I'm not going to hang on anybody's cross.

FELICIA: But whether you want to be a role model or not, you now are.

JOHN: I'm not taking responsibility for it.

FELICIA: But you *have* it; what are you going to *do* with it?

JOHN: I'm going to ignore it.

FELICIA: It's impossible.

JOHN (coldly): Not for me . . .

The more Felicia backed John into a corner, the more flustered he became, but when she asked him if he thought his kids would rebel against *him,* it produced the liveliest, most earnest response of the show. "I hope so!" he said. "I don't want my kids to grow up to be just like me. I want them to be themselves, I want them to have some independence. If they don't rebel against me, I'll think something is the matter . . . When people stop rebelling against what is set up as true, then we might as well all lay down and die!"

Here was the quintessential John Cougar, the most crystalline articulation of what he was all about. The notion of rebellion, not for rebellion sake but as a means of enhancing and reconfirming life, was what drove him, what lay behind his anger, his music, his developing vision. Jeter had touched her subject's rawest nerve. But instead of taking the conversation to much more revealing depths, she made the fatal mistake of bringing it back to the same question: "You are now the person you were rebelling against a few years ago. And what are you going to do with that?"

For a moment, watching John sit there—head bent painfully forward, elbows on knees, the current of tension visibly clenching in his jaws—it seemed that he was going to smash her. As John later delicately put it, "I think she had women's lib and being a bitch all mixed up!" At that instant, this unsuspecting journalist represented every authority figure in his life who ever tried to shoehorn him into being something that he hated: ". . . you're a taxpayer, a homeowner . . ." (Are you right with the program yet, Luke? Get back down in that ditch and keep diggin'!). His control snapped ike a twig, and the good old Bad Mellencamp Family Attitude reared its head.

"Now, wait a minute!" he sputtered. "I do *not* attend PTA meetings! I do *not* attend the Nazarene Church! I do *not* take part in any of that stuff . . ."

Taken aback by the outburst, all that Felicia could think to say was, "You pay car insurance . . ."

"I've had car insurance since I was eighteen!"

"You're a *daddy . . .*"

John called time like a referee, ripped off his mike, and stopped the proceedings. "I don't want to *(expletive)* on TV and argue with you . . ."

Felicia wasn't about to let him walk off her show so easily—it was its first

"You are now the person you were rebelling against a few years ago . . ."

week of airing. She would face politicians, famous authors, movie stars, and she wasn't about to be snubbed by some snot-nosed rock star. She tried to lure him back with some conciliatory palaver, but John wasn't having any of it. Of course, John made the mistake of assuming that the cameras had been turned off, that the *Nightwatch* people would only air the first few segments, but this was irresistible theater of the real. "I hope these cameras aren't still running," he said lamely—then realized that they were. "Howard!" he called off to his right, a hopeless plea for help. Bloom stood off camera, pacing nervously around the panic-stricken Vicky Mellencamp.

"We aren't doing anything unusual," Felicia said, now trying to assuage her steaming guest. "You haven't really changed the fabric of the American thinking . . ."

"Howard!"

Before anyone could say another word, John walked off the platform set and skulked off into the studio like a fugitive, the camera stalking him until he disappeared into the darkness.

Was it all worth it in the end? The struggles in the studio, with his record company, with his manager, with the bad reviews, with the endless touring. Certainly, the first time he saw a playback of the episode of *Nightwatch,* he didn't think so. He was lying flat on his back in a hotel room in Buffalo, dead tired after the show, hands clasped behind his head; he flicked on his old friend Mr. TV to relax and there it was, the whole humiliating rigamarole. "All I could do," he says, "was close my eyes and grimace and pray for it to go away . . ."

But all the while, "Hurts So Good" kept moving up the charts until it hit the top slot and roosted there for twelve weeks. "Jack and Diane" climbed almost as quickly, nudging into the Top Ten right behind it. All summer long, from Carmel to Canarsie, the songs poured forth from car radios, from Walkmans and ghetto blasters, flavoring the lives of tens of millions of people. During the first week of September 1982, *American Fool* jumped two notches and knocked Fleetwood Mac's *Mirage* out of the top spot to become, for nine glorious weeks, the biggest-selling LP in the United States. *Chestnut Street Incident* had sold a total of twelve thousand copies; *American Fool* was selling that many in just half a day. "When the album went platinum it was kind of like a dream," Mike Wanchic relates. "We laughed about it: What the fuck *is* this? *Us?* Number *One?* Then we played the Market Square Arena in Indianapolis and 18,500 people were going nuts before we even hit the stage— you couldn't hear the PA it was so loud! That's when it started to sink in . . ."

On the day "Hurts So Good" went No. 1, John and Vicky invited everybody over for cake and champagne. "There was ozone in the air that day," Vicky Mellencamp remembers, "you could feel it. Everybody kept walking around, kind of dazed, saying, 'Can you believe it?' John kept saying, 'It feels kind of *weird* . . .' "

It would get much more bizarre, of course, but for the time being John Cougar was much too exhausted to pay attention, too spent to even begin coming to grips with the myriad changes that were overtaking him and transforming his life with the passing days. Before his Grammy, before his American Music Award, the only satisfaction he allowed himself was the not insignificant pleasure of knowing that he would once again be able to call himself by his real name—Mellencamp. For the time being, he was content to luxuriate in the knowledge that he didn't have to get up and go anywhere, that he would soon be coming into a rather hefty amount of cash. "For whatever it was worth," he laughs, "I had worked out at least one of my original goals: I really could just put my feet up, drink Big Red, and watch as much TV as I liked!"—he remained oblivious to everything else. Even when large groups of liquored-up kids started turning up outside his house late at night to bellow, *"Hey Cougar! Come on out and party! Hey, rock and roooooooll!"*—he would wake up only long enough to groan, roll over, and go right back to sleep.

V

*J*OHN *C*OUGAR *M*ELLENCAMP

Wherein the Kid Inside Grows Up Even More, Kicks a Sleeping Dog, Says Uh-Huh for the Last Time, and Ponders the Golden Gates

"Success gives you a different kind of freedom in your career, but not in your private life. I still can't believe that people recognize me. Don't get me wrong, I know that that's all part of the business, but when I'm standing at a urinal and someone says, 'Give me your autograph'—well, 'What hand do you want me to use?' "

American Fool was the bestselling album of 1982, at sales of about 3 million units. If you compare this to the 5-million-plus sales figures for other megasellers and the accrual of royalties for artists over the years, you can see how depressed the music industry actually was during the Year of Cougar. The LP that carried him over the hump was really small potatoes when you ponder the 25 million units of Michael Jackson's *Thriller,* with its earnings of roughly $75 million for its artist, not to mention what CBS managed to abscond with. And yet, after seven fallow, furious—at times humiliating—years in the music business that often seemed to approach the proportions of a Shakespearean comedy of errors, the result was undeniable: John Cougar Mellencamp had *made* it. On his own terms, no less. Why, the effects of his personal life and career were mind-boggling . . .

Consider! It meant, firstly, fame: "Sometimes lately, I've been tempted to start drinking again, which is something I haven't thought about in ten years," John revealed to Lynn Van Matre of the *Chicago Tribune,* "because it's real hard to relax and all this crazy stuff keeps happening!" *Crazy stuff* meant going out to the Ponderosa Steak House and being surrounded by sixty people—"None of my friends want to go out and eat with me now," he would say—or having twenty people pull into your driveway every day who just want to say hello, or the kids following you around the mall in Bloomington while you buy Pampers for the baby with Vicky. It meant not being able to go out to shoot pool someplace or to play at a bar in town; once John played a bar in Bloomington, at the Bluebird, under the name COPS—Cougar Out Playing Secretly. It meant people coming out of the woodwork of your past—obscure people who really didn't like you that much—asking favors, like, "Hey, John, I got this tape, see?" Suddenly, his family and old buddies became oracles of information about him, sought after by the media. There was his old buddy Mark Ripley, smiling quizzically as he pointed out where Marilyn's Coffee Shop used to be on Chestnut Street, for the cameras of the Columbus *Dispatch;* and brother Joe, now a reputable engineer, married with a couple of kids in Columbus, being phoned by reporters and telling them, "Hey, I've got to set the record straight . . . Ever since John became famous, everybody around here thinks I'm some kind of a hoodlum or something, and I'm not!" It meant Marilyn Mellencamp holding forth in her living room to *People* magazine. It meant security systems and double locks and the strange, disorienting isolation that comes to people who experience that first rush of celebrity in America—a ceaseless onslaught of people and events coming full-tilt at you, turning your head around and filling you with tension until you reach the breaking point, which happened to John while standing on a streetcorner in Seymour with his brother Ted. A group of high school kids rode by, recognized him, and shouted, "Hey, I'd like to stomp John Cougar's ass!" "I had to stop myself from taking off after them, I was so mad," John says. "It really blew my mind to realize how those kids could push my buttons like that. That's when I knew I had to step back and take it easy and take a good look at it all . . ."

What makes fame so surreal is that the world seems at your feet and at your throat at the same time. Girls meet you and offer to perform fellatio under tables, behind trees, just because of *who you are* (or who they *think* you are); they want carnal knowledge of you in the worst of ways—sexual autographs,

(Harvey Wang)

if you will. On the other hand, people resent your success and look for opportunities to bring you down. "I get really paranoid," John told *Indianapolis Magazine* in April of 1983. "You never know when someone is going to punch you out! You don't know what people are going to do . . ."

John quickly learned that success was a tool, and that he had to be discerning about using it. When Fort Wayne asked him to do a free concert for the flood volunteers who had filled a million sandbags to hold back the city's swollen rivers, he was more than happy to comply. On the other hand, when the Seymour Chamber of Commerce offered to put up a sign on the interstate reading WELCOME TO SEYMOUR: BIRTHPLACE OF JOHN COUGAR MELLENCAMP—but *only* under the stipulation that he do a benefit to raise money for the town—he declined. "It seemed like they were trying to make a trade with him," says Mark Ripley, "and it turned him off. You know, a few years before John'd had a few Grammy nominations, and it wasn't even mentioned in the local Seymour papers. John's attitude was, 'If I'm going to do a benefit, I'll do it for people who really deserve it, like the unemployed steelworkers.' "

Next came the money, paid by Polygram in installments to Billy Gaff, trickling down to John in ever-increasing sums. "When 'Hurts So Good' went Number One," remembers Gary Boebinger, "John said to me, 'Boy, in about a year, I'm gonna have more money than I know what to do with!' " Oddly, the money seemed to be almost secondary in importance to John. Sure, he bought a few nifty cars and bikes and made plans to buy a bigger place outside of Bloomington, but his tastes were simple—how many leather jackets can you own?—the money was put away for future projects. Mostly, the money meant that John could play benefactor to friends and family alike—he became, in essence, a sort of First National Bank of Mellencamp—and to donate to whatever charity he saw fit. Of course, gifts were happily dispensed, like the surprise Harley-Davidson that he sent to Bill Cataldo at his home in Nutley, New Jersey, for his hard work on *American Fool*. Initially, the money produced an easement of tension and anxiety in John, a kind of childlike awe. "When it first started happening," Mark Ripley observes, "he became like a little kid in a candy store saying, 'Let's see what I can get away with here!' " Before long, euphoria gave way to financial sobriety, a kind of down-to-earth pragmatism about what money could and couldn't do. John wasn't about to go off the deep end of wild extravagance and hedonistic self-indulgence. He began to see how lucky he was that it had taken him so long to make it. "Boy, I'm glad I wasn't nineteen years old when it happened," he says. "I'd probably have blown my brains out! Because it took so long to build, I was able to see it for what it really was."

What it really was to John Cougar Mellencamp was a chance to do what he'd always wanted: simply to make the best possible music for the people who wanted to listen. For one thing, he realized that the best part of his work had always been closest to the source, closest to home. Thus, precisely at the time in his career when he could have uprooted himself and moved anywhere in the world, he resolved to stay exactly where he was—in Bloomington, surrounded by those he knew best, where about the biggest thing that ever happens is Homecoming Weekend. "I know when I was a kid I couldn't wait to get out of here," he reflects. "I guess I started realizing that I get my strength from my roots. Indiana's my home and everybody I love is here. I actually stay home a lot—I'm pretty reclusive by nature. I decided to just live and work here—write songs and record them about very basic, human emotions. If people like the music that comes out of this, well, then, that's great."

His attitude about his work was evolving, a process hastened by the realization that millions of people had really listened to the words of his songs. "As corny as 'Oh yeah, life goes on, long after the thrill of living is gone' is, I had so many people come up and tell me how much those lines meant to them. One guy told me that, after his wife's father had died, he played her the song and she was really comforted by that line. I mean, that wasn't how I wrote them. I thought they were just a couple of dumb lines I jotted off, but the fact that they were a comfort like that was important. It really opened my eyes."

In the wake of *American Fool,* John wanted to find out as much as he could about who had liked the record and why. He commissioned a hard-hitting radio study by Bill Hard that assessed everything from his demographic market to how people reacted to his image. "We got back responses from over a hundred stations," Hard remembers, "and we sat down and went over them all. I think he had been so blindsided as a kid in the business by other people's ambitions and machinations that he now realized that knowledge is power, and he needed that power to keep from being manipulated. He's a real quick-study artist, and he knows how to keep his finger on the pulse. He learned how publishing works, record company politics, how radio works—and, finally, how the music public was perceiving him."

As if to remind John of where he had come from and how far he had traveled, MainMan released *The Kid Inside* right on the heels of *American Fool,* to ride the coat tails of its success. Tony DeFries was certainly within his contractual rights, but what seemed insupportable was his failure to clearly designate the record as an artifact—an obvious ploy to mislead the public into buying the record as new product. Amazingly, several rock critics fell right into the trap, accepting the record as the followup to *American Fool,* using the occasion to lambaste John, making complete fools of themselves in the process. John's attitude was stoical; he called the record "unmusical" and "prehistoric": "I'd just hate to have some kid pay $9.95 for a record I made when I was twenty-three years old, and be disappointed," he told the *Night Rock News.* Of course, what really hurt was having that embarrassing lip-gloss photo—the one that Jamie Andrews did in Marilyn Monroe's shower at the Hotel Lexington—come out after all those years. "At least I'm not on the cover with a dress," John remarked to *Stereo Review,* "like that ancient LP that DeFries pulled out of his vaults and released on David Bowie!" As it turned out, DeFries's release got very little airplay and sold sparsely. "There was a real backlash toward it when people realized what it was," notes Bill Hard. "I remember deciding not to write about it in my tipsheet because I felt it was a real lowball move and didn't want to give it publicity. I felt that MainMan had really used John as a kid; now that he was finally starting to get someplace, give the guy a break!"

Even if *The Kid Inside* had never appeared, John Cougar Mellencamp would have remained down to earth about the meaning of his success. After all, there were still a lot of people who remained unconvinced of his talent. In the 1982 *Rolling Stone* Reader's Poll, for example, he came in third, behind both Springsteen and the Clash. What *American Fool* had really done was open a door of opportunity to establish his longevity as an artist. Perhaps the most wondrous thing about his new situation was his autonomy, his independence; precisely because he had made it despite what everybody—critics and record company—had predicted, he was beholden to nobody in the business. As long as he maintained the trust and respect of his segment of the music-loving public, he could continue to do what he wanted, thumbing his nose at everything else, making no compromises. For this very reason, he turned down all the offers for commercial endorsements that flooded in after *American Fool,* many of them highly lucrative propositions from companies like Camel and Nike. "It would have been very easy money," he recognizes, "and one day I may be sorry I turned them down, but I didn't want to owe anything to any corporation."

On the other hand, the very freedom inherent in his new situation gave rise to a whole new set of challenges, questions, and anxieties—all of them deriving from that old adage of not wishing for something too much because you just might get it. For many individuals who attain a degree of stardom, the problem becomes one of maintenance and growth, which is a different ball game than simply getting there. He now had new questions to ask himself:

How do I keep it from slipping away? What do I do next? What if I blow it?
With his background, John had few illusions about the music business or
doubts about its constant, devouring hunger for novelties and trends. As he
put it, "I knew 'Hurts So Good' would get old pretty fast. How could I expect
it *not* to get old for my audience when it gets old for *me?*" At the same time,
he had learned the invaluable lesson that all he could do was to be himself;
that, as Woody Guthrie once said, "All you can write is what you see." His
next step became delineated: to demonstrate real growth as a songwriter in
the scope and theme of his work. "Always in the back of my mind," he says,
"was the feeling that if I just kept getting better and better at what I did,
everything else would work itself out." To accomplish this on his next record,
he would move even closer to his musical and cultural roots, but not before a
side trip, a detour into another project.

Mitch Ryder was born William Levise, Jr., some forty years ago. His heyday
in music came from 1965 to 1967, when he fronted the Detroit Wheels,
recording such hits as "Devil with a Blue Dress On," "Good Golly Miss
Molly," "Sock It to Me, Baby," and "Jenny, Take a Ride," a celebrated
fusing of Little Richard's "Jenny Jenny" with Chuck Willis's "C.C. Rider."
These songs had sent shivers down John Mellencamp's spine when he heard
them on the radio in Seymour; in interviews over the years he had often
acknowledged Ryder's influence on him, saying things like, "Mitch Ryder
taught my generation how to rock." But Mitch Ryder's story was an unhappy
one. For one thing, Ryder simply had not been pretty enough to make it big in
the pop music world of the mid-1960s and his subsequent records never
caught fire. By the mid-1970s, it was pretty much over for him in the United
States; and like many other American "legends" who can't find work in their
own country, he released four albums in Europe, playing clubs and concerts
wherever possible. When John did an interview at a Detroit radio station with
a DJ who knew Ryder and once again talked about Ryder's influence on him,
the DJ gave Ryder his number. "I called John and we talked, and I told him I
was working on an LP for Europe," Ryder later told WISH-TV in Louisville.
"He said he'd send me some tapes and he sent down two, and I called back
and told him I really liked them. He said, 'Well, I've got a better idea. Instead
of just doing the songs, why don't you let me produce you?' I said, 'Why
not?' "
    Polygram agreed to the project and signed Ryder to his first American
record deal in a long while. After all, John had proven himself as a producer;
moreover, there seemed to be a developing trend for younger artists produc-

ing their idols of yesteryear; Springsteen had produced Gary U.S. Bonds and Tom Petty, Del Shannon. But given the intensity of John, the producer, and Ryder, artist, the collaboration was destined to be a volatile one. As one observer at a preproduction meeting put it, "The record could be great, if they make it out of the studio alive."

Never Kick a Sleeping Dog was recorded at the "Shack," an unfinished farmhouse outside of Brownstown in the middle of miles of cornfields, which John had converted into a rough studio with a mobile recording unit from Criteria. The band consisted of Larry Crane on guitar, Ken Aronoff on drums, and Ryder's bass player, Mark Gougeon. The working atmosphere was sometimes smooth, sometimes tense. "Mitch used to have these wild breakfasts," John recalls, "like, a Twinkie, a beef jerky, and a warm Budweiser. I used to love listening to his stories. Boy, I thought I'd had some rocky times in this business; but when I realized what *he'd* been through, I realized I'd had it pretty easy! He had real horror stories . . ."

The conflicts between the two stemmed from their expectations of each other and of the record. "The only disagreements we had were for the betterment of the album," Ryder later explained to the *Detroit Free Press*. "Cougar had to forget he was a singer. In the beginning, he was listening to every note I was singing. I felt a bit smothered. He wanted me to sing what his perception of Mitch Ryder was. He had to get in tune with my perspective. If we hadn't gotten complete control, it could've been a John Cougar record. Finally, he backed off . . . He was able to overcome his artistic personality, his emotion. He didn't surprise me. When I saw that boy work in the studio, I knew he was a producer . . ."

John quickly realized that he was dealing with a painfully insecure personality who was always worried about losing control of a record. "I think he was afraid because he saw it as his one last break," John told *Creem* after the record was completed, "and I don't see it that way at all. It's just another page in the Mitch Ryder story, because he's the type of guy who's never going away and that's the truth. He doesn't know that about himself, but it's the truth . . ."

The three standout songs on the record were suggested by the producer, all of them tailor-made for Ryder's whiskey-soaked baritone and raucous delivery—a voice that sounds its best and most natural when it attains the sonority of a backed-up vacuum cleaner revving at high speed. Keith Sykes's "Bigtime" detonates with maximum force, only to be eclipsed by Ryder's cover of Prince's "When You Were Mine," which John thought was one of the most perfect rock songs ever written. "That's got to be the best track I've

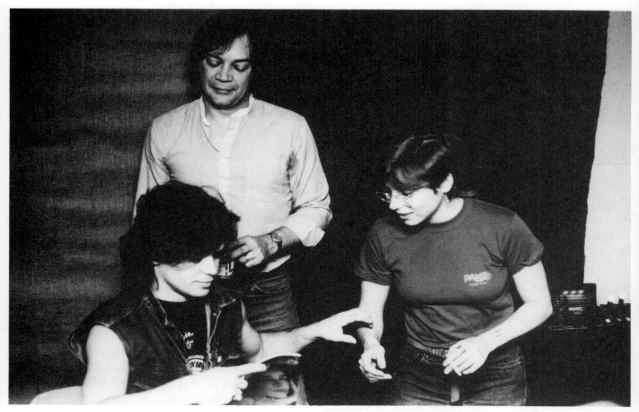

Mitch Ryder and Go-Go's drummer Gina Shock with John at the Shack.

ever played on in my life," Larry Crane marvels. "The take was absolute magic." The result was a quintessentially 1980s song performed by a quintessentially 1960s singer, rendered in the spare, high-contrast style of *American Fool*—a metallic wall of rhythm guitars, punctured by Aronoff's drums caroming off the walls of the Shack, pierced by a vocal performance that in texture and energy is the equal of anything in Mitch Ryder's career. The big surprise on the album was Mitch's duet with Marianne Faithfull, another relic of the 1960s pop scene who was making a comeback, on B. Amesbury's "A Thrill's a Thrill," a ballad that Long John Baldry had recorded years earlier. The Baldry version had been a song ostensibly about sexual thrills, but with the low, scratchy interplay of these two voices, the song became a naked, true-life statement about the whole rock & roll life-style, sung by two people who had weathered it all over twenty years. The album contained a few other strong cuts ("Cry to Me," "Come Again"), but nothing quite approached the level of these songs.

When the American Music Awards asked John to appear on the 1983 show, he agreed, but only with the stipulation that he could take Mitch Ryder on the show, to give his record a good launching. On the night of the telecast, John showed up in a three-month-old beard—"I was going through the thing of being recognized all the time and hating it, so I grew a beard to hide behind"— jeans ripped out at both knees, sneakers, a T-shirt, and a Levis jacket that looked like the original Levi had worn it and buried it for about a hundred years. "You're not *really* going out there like that," Bill Cataldo said to him backstage, "are you?" "Of course I am," John said indignantly. "What did they expect me to wear—a *tuxedo?*"

They performed "Bigtime" with Mitch so nervous that he kept listing to one side like a drunkard and John looking like some wild, exotic species of Appalachian mountain devil. Like his last performance on the show, when he performed "Ain't Even Done with the Night," people gaped and applauded politely at the end. When called back to the podium to accept his award for Favorite Pop Male, John mystified people even more by saying, "Hey, what can I say, I'm an idiot, thanks a lot . . . ," and scurrying away before anybody could clap. "People just didn't know how to take him," recalls Russel Shaw. "I thought it was funny but nobody took it that way. People from the press and record company, even his publicist, came up to me and said, 'Why did he have to *say* that?' "

At least this time there was no vomiting, no thudding palpitations in his chest that required a trip to the hospital after the show. John merely looked at himself in the mirror and promptly shaved off his beard. The next day, he was heading back to Indiana, thinking about his next album.

The songs came fast when they came, setting both the theme and style. "One day I was driving back from the Indianapolis airport on a highway elevated about forty feet above the ground," John recalls, "and I looked down and saw this old man sitting in his backyard in front of a pink house, with a dog in his arms staring up at me with this real contented look on his face. It was obvious that he was content with his life, but there he was with a damned six-lane highway running through his backyard!"

It burst on him like some shocking realization, like an abrupt change of weather, that he had been living smack dab in the middle of an America for his entire life—"the kind of America that you never see on postcards," as he would later describe it—that he could now write about with the kind of emotional intimacy and critical distance that might reveal something about the

With Marianne Faithfull, listening to a playback of "A Thrill's A Thrill."

way we live and think and feel. He began to understand fully that his best material was as much an organic part of his life as the lines on his grandfather's face, or the blue of his little daughter's eyes—as every memory or aspiration in the history of his family. He could write about it and never have to worry any more that it wasn't as good as Dylan or Springsteen or anybody else—because the fact that it was coming out of him only made it more singular, more real.

There's a black man with a black cat living in a
    black neighborhood
He's got an interstate running through his front yard
You know he thinks he's got it so good
And there's a woman in the kitchen cleaning up the
    evening slop
And he looks at her and he says, 'Darlin' I can
    remember when you could stop a clock'

He knew this place well—a land where "those old crazy dreams just kind of came and went," not the land of "winners and losers," or of people working in some "high rise," vacationing down at "the Gulf of Mexico," but a place of "greasy hair" and "greasy smiles," where "the simple man, baby, pays for the thrills, the bills, the pills that kill." The chorus was a rousing blend of patriotic irony, a populist gem of American ambiguity; had Woody Guthrie been alive in the Indiana of the 1980s, he might have conjured something very similar.

Oh but ain't that America for you and me
Ain't that America were something to see, baby
Ain't that America, home of the free
Little pink houses for you and me

"Pink Houses" created a kind of volition, an energy of its own, that would set the tone for the whole project. In July, John called Don Gehman and once again rigged the Shack for recording, turning the kitchen into the control room. Most artists would agonize over the followup record to a breakthrough, multiplatinum LP—the pressure to equal or exceed the performance of the hit album is monumental—but John's idea was to capture a spirit, to have fun, to capitalize on the most spontaneous qualities of the songwriter and band in a kind of rock & roll blitzkrieg. John Mellencamp simply refused to take the easy route and make a followup album to *American Fool,* with the kind of teen-oriented songs that had made him famous. For sixteen straight days, with his band virtually living in the Shack, they worked straight through, recording fifteen songs, at a trifling cost of $100,000 (*American Fool* had cost almost three times that much). Some songs were written at midnight, recorded the next day in two hours, with vocals recorded the first time through. "Don't let me go back and touch *any* of these songs, even if I want to," John told Gehman and the band.

"It was the first time we had enough confidence not to ruin the tracks," says Mike Wanchic. "So many times in the past, we'd get a great basic track and ruin it by erasing and overdubbing until it sounded really overwrought. We wanted to catch everything possible—even the flaws." "Musically, John hears everything in his head," bassist Toby Myers relates of the sessions, "but he can't execute it. He and Larry have a real mental highway between them because they've been together for so long; Larry assimilates the basic rhythm of the song, and we sit there silently until Larry makes a few passes and then we start adding really basic stuff, cautiously, until it grows. Sometimes, it just falls right in."

The music was a throwback to those Rolling Stones records of the mid- to late 1960s that John had grown up with in Seymour, a snarling mixture of Larry Crane's acoustic and Mike Wanchic's tinny electric guitars that sounded like it was recorded in a garage, Aronoff's drums now sounding like an amalgamation of tin cans and trash bins. Behind this thick, dirty rock & roll sound, however, were subtle intonations of country rock on "Pink Houses" and "Authority Song," as well as R&B and folk.

Assorted axware at the Shack used for *Uh Huh*.

(Lance Staedler/Courtesy Polygram)

Toby Myers, John, and Don Gehman during the sixteen day marathon.

"Pink Houses" was recorded in two days. The song features a breezy, countrified instrumental break, with the band joining John on the final verses to shout "Huh!"—which conjures the soul backing on Sam Cooke's "Chain Gang," while John rears back and launches into the most impassioned singing of his career. Other songs were filled with that sardonic, self-mocking Mellencamp humor. In "The Authority Song," which evokes Bobby Fuller's "I Fought the Law," he manages to encapsulate his lifelong revolt in a single ditty—"I been doing it since I was a young kid and I've come out grinnin' . . ."—but, naturally, "Authority always wins."

In "Round Five" John asks the preacher for strength to fight, to which the preacher tells him, "Grow up, son." John informs him, "Growing up leads to growing old and then to dying,/And dying to me don't sound like all that much fun."

"Play Guitar," written with a local hairstylist named Dan Ross, who'd given John and Ted and the band their wild rockabilly duck tails, was designed as a satirical homage to the time-honored, adolescent notion that playing rock & roll could make you cool, get you girls, put the world at your feet. "Forget all about that macho *shit*," John shouts—knowing full well that he would later

have to punch in *stuff* for *shit* should the song ever be played on the radio—
"and learn how to play guitah!" The song shows the band as the perfect
garage quintet, with Larry Crane sawing away on the chords from "Gloria"—
obligatory fare for any high school band during the 1960s—on what turned out
to be one of the nastiest, greasiest guitar breaks of the year.

Perhaps the purest incarnation of the Stones, circa *Exile on Main Street,* on
the record was "Serious Business," which returned John to the theme of the
music business but seen from the new vantage point of success ("I've come
this far and I can't go back"). Everything is being served to him on a silver
platter, but the price tag attached ("Take my life/Take my soul/Put me on the
cross for all to see") is serious business indeed, even if what he's trafficking in
is nothing but "sex and violence and rock & roll."

Finally, at the very end of the album, came "Golden Gates," or what John
referred to as the DB—"designated ballad." The song was put together almost
as an afterthought, and yet it embodies all that he had come to learn about his
values. The message is delivered from a perspective that is stripped of
illusion—"Ain't no golden gates gonna swing open/Ain't no streets paved in
natural pearl"—at a time of "uncertain futures" for everybody, from a place
divorced from the "big deals" of the "masters" and "authorities"—"Got
nothing to do with me and you." In the end, nothing matters but people, love,
the sincerity of true human emotion: "The only promises that I know to be
true/Are the promises made from the heart."

After sixteen days, John took the tapes to New York to get feedback from a
few select people; he came back realizing that the record needed one more
song, a real kicker. "He told me that he wasn't satisfied with anything for the
single," remembers George Green. "I'd written six to eight lines about
'crumbling walls' and read it to him over the phone; he copied it down and
worked with it. I went over to his house that night and we wrote the second
verse. Later, when he played it for me, it was weird because it was so wordy!
I kept thinking, 'Where's the *choruses?*' "

"Crumblin' Down," recorded in one night at TRC in Indianapolis, was a
major departure from "Hurts So Good." Musically, the song once again
dipped into the wealth of primal rock & roll sources and found its identity in
what John called "the slop bucket" of ragged, early 1960s R&B; but lyrically,
the song was a self-portrait, an onslaught, a scathing tongue lashing.

> Some people say I'm obnoxious and lazy
> That I'm uneducated and my opinion means nothin'
> But I know I'm a real good dancer . . .

"It's hard to say what that song means," Green offers. "People thought John was expressing that it wasn't such a big deal being a rock star—you know, *Here I am, and so what?* The feeling we worked with is, "What are you going to do when it's over, when the big time deal falls through? 'I'll be here, how about you?' " "That was a very nervy song," comments Chris Connelly, "because he addressed himself in a way that not many artists have tried to do—people think these things about me, and this is how I feel about it. It's a hard song to write . . ."

The new album was called *Uh-Huh,* a reference to all of the times in John's life that he had acquiesced to people's suggestions against his better judgment and had gotten screwed for it. It featured a painting of John on the cover looking impossibly callow, surrounded by a couple of funky angels with little devil's tails between their legs; inside was a photo of John and the band dining grossly on Kentucky Fried Chicken and watermelon amid pigs rooting in the mud of sister Laura's pig farm in Seymour. (John is roaring with laughter, having just dumped one of the Colonel's buckets over Ken Aronoff's head.) It had taken him almost a decade to do so, but he finally reclaimed his family name on the record and became, professionally, *John Cougar Mellencamp.* To friends, family, and the people in the music business who knew him, the symbolism in the name change was obvious: John Mellencamp had come

Lining up a shot for "Pink Houses" in Austin.

home to himself. "Well, I'd love to even phase the *Cougar* out of it," John told Lisa Robinson on Radio 1990, "except the record company would absolutely go out of their minds . . ."

Keeping the *Cougar* turned out to be just about the only nod toward the institutional authority of the record company that John would have to make. Many of the old powers at Polygram had been swept away since *American Fool;* things were vastly different now that his record sales were paying the record company's phone bills. Consider the playback session for *Uh-Huh,* designed for single selection: "He went through the motion of inviting the A&R people for a session at Cherokee after the album was mixed," Jerry Jaffe recollects, "and everyone left thinking that they'd had some input as to what the first, second, and third single would be, but he subtley manipulated the whole thing. Everyone left thinking, 'Isn't it *nice* how John opened it up to the record company?' but the whole thing was a setup!"

Likewise, the videos were nearly perfect actualizations of Mellencamp concepts. Both "Pink Houses" and "Crumblin' Down," which marked the apogee of his association with producer Simon Fields, were put together in conjunction with a half-hour show for a new documentary series on Cinemax called *Album Flash,* which presented a near-lethal production deadline for the pieces. Considering the speed with which they were shot and assembled—people on the production crew, who referred to that time as the "Indiana Death March," were literally averaging about an hour of sleep a night—the pieces are remarkable.

"Crumblin' Down," shot at the auditorium of Indiana University, was John's first truly organic performance piece—conceived, choreographed, and staged by John in a way that sought to eliminate all barriers between himself and the camera. Seated sullenly in a simple chair at the outset, with feet tapping spasmodically and cigarette in hand—the video would start a minor fashion craze for black Bass Weejuns with white socks and jeans ripped out in the knees—he falls out of the chair after the first verse into a paroxysm of dancing, leapfrogging over parking meters into a hard-floor split, sliding down a long ladder in one fell swoop. The video was shot over the course of a single evening, but the hours dragged far into the morning. With each take, John just kept coming harder and harder at the camera.

"Pink Houses" was a documentary-style rendering of the song through beautiful pastel images of the grandeur and decay of small-town southern Indiana—its fields, railroad, farms, roads, and people—all of it shot around Seymour and outlying places like Austin and Little York. Things fell nicely into place as the crew went about grabbing images: John found his actual pink house in Austin, and his old black man materialized in the form of Joe Todd, an eighty-three-year-old resident of a Madison nursing home. The snorting, charging buffalo were contributed by John Morgan of Austin's Morgan Packing Company, and the lanky hillbilly dancing bare-chested with the straw hat on the porch at the end was no less a local celebrity than Austin Mayor Harvey Gooden. The video became an event, and everywhere John went with the crew, they attracted crowds of enthusiasts. While they were filming a night shot at Little York, one biker even took it upon himself to control the crowd and to protect John's Corvette by casually whipping out a pistol and planting himself on its hood. "You think anybody asked *him* to move?" John laughs. "No way!"

Many people saw the "Pink Houses" video as an unabashed patriotic paean when it was released, no doubt because of the American flag billowing gloriously in the breeze during the instrumental break. "It's not rah-rah America," John demurs. "There's a lot of Americana in it, but it's really trying to say, Let's take a good look at ourselves. Maybe the American Dream isn't what it's cracked up to be . . ."

Several White House aides who later screened the video didn't see it that way, however, perhaps relating the images to Ronald Reagan's Midwestern upbringing. When they contacted John and expressed an interest in showing the president the piece, perhaps using it for his 1984 reelection effort, John refused. "I didn't mind it being sent to the president," he explained. "In fact, I was flattered. But there was no way I wanted it used for political purposes." "People around here were kind of flabbergasted when he did that," relates Gary Boebinger. "Around here, no matter what side of the fence you're on, when the President of the United States asks you for something, you do it without questions. But not John Mellencamp. He had a good laugh about it . . ."

With advance orders of over half a million, *Uh-Huh* shipped gold and went platinum within five weeks of its release; the video for "Crumblin' Down," with its smoky lighting and Mellencamp shuffle, went into immediate high rotation at MTV, followed by "Pink Houses." Now, instead of having to beg, borrow, and steal to get on *Saturday Night Live,* John Cougar Mellencamp was booked on the season's opener, where he performed those two songs with backup singers Pat Peterson and Carol Sue Hill bedecked in red cheerleader's outfits. Although sales of the LP would eventually outstrip *American Fool*'s, the record reached its zenith on the *Billboard* chart on January 28, 1984, at No. 9 with a bullet; "Crumblin' Down," "Pink Houses," and "Authority Song" reached Nos. 9, 8, and 15 on the singles charts, respectively. More important and gratifying this time was the media response to the record. A sea change had clearly taken place in the press since *American Fool,* perhaps best expressed by the title of Deborah Frost's perceptive cover story in the *Record:* "The Kid's Alright." "This was no ignorant, arrogant—or just plain lucky—country bumpkin," Frost wrote of John, after watching him film the "Crumblin' Down" video. "Perhaps it's as easy to misread his statements (as when he told *Rolling Stone* that writing songs was just like getting a hard-on—what he meant was if you think about it too much it won't come) and his actions . . . as to misinterpret his deceptively simple songs. Cougar likes to tell tales. He also likes to argue, as everyone (including himself) will tell you. Where he comes from, there ain't much else to do."

While several of the heavies of rock criticism still remained cautiously aloof and unconvinced, the general reaction to the album was one of unanimous enthusiasm. *Playboy* wrote: "Cougar has cut some of the swagger out of his songs and has hit upon a hacksaw simplicity that makes his one of the smartest voices in the land between Flatbush and the Basin." *People* contributed: "Mellencamp has refined his writing to the point where his songs are not just emotional honks but little tales full of the vagaries of life." *Rolling Stone,* after its acerbic pan of *American Fool,* now lauded John for his "humor and untamed spirit," for his "cat-burglar adroitness for pinching fretboard riffs from a wealth of primal rock & roll sources," and pronounced the record a "collection of brash, full-throttle rockers."

"Most of the critics waited and reserved judgment about John," remarks Polygram's Sherry Ring Ginsberg. "They waited to see if it was cool to like him." The perception of John Mellencamp in the press—the same media bandwagon that had once viewed him as a bad caricature of somebody else—had now, for the most part, about-faced to embrace him with open arms. At a time when pop music was being inundated with new bands from England hawking fashions and technopop, he found himself in the vanguard of a group of artists making purely American, roots-oriented rock. Moreover, by explicitly embracing real social issus, he had radically transformed his image from a good-time, macho rocker to a tough-minded observer of the real world.

" 'Crumblin' Down' was partly inspired by my thirty-eight-year-old cousin in Indiana," John explained to the New York *Daily News.* "He's an electrical worker who's been on the bench [unemployed] for over a year now. This guy's spirit is being broken by America, and that's crazy, because he loves this country, and he works so hard. I've been lucky, I know that. But there are a lot of people, people close to me, who haven't been lucky, and I'd rather write about them than me. . . . It's a very frightening thing when you realize that the industrial revolution is over and there's no place to go."

"Pink Houses," as openended as the lyrics were, struck a deep chord at a

At sister Laura's pig farm in Dudleyville: (left to right) Aronoff, Mellencamp, Myers, Wanchic, and Crane.

time of deepening recession in the smokestack industries of the Midwest, at a time of mounting farm crises, deracination, and alienation. "Rock and roll loves voices from Nowhere," noted Christopher Hill in the *Record*, "and a good part of the Middle Western part of this country is Nowhere." Observing that this was John's "first conscious effort to speak collectively for the people of his state and his state of mind," Hill concluded that "anyone who thinks it's worth it to try to speak for a whole subculture . . . obviously has a vision which sees beyond blasted hopes and wasted self-indulgence. . . . And precisely because Mellencamp's not purveying working class oratorios to college kids—because in important ways, he is his audience—it's a vision that might make a difference." Similarly, in a *Village Voice* piece called "Jack and Diane Get Pissed Off," Lee Ballinger, like John a native of southern Indiana, hailed *Uh-Huh*'s populist spirit: "The continuing polarization of wealth and power in the 1980s will provide similar opportunities for John Mellencamp and any other performer who wants to make more than music."

"Maybe I am a spokesman for the little guy, but I sure wish there was somebody smarter than me doing it," John told Zach Dunkin of the *Indianapolis Times*. "I'm just a dumb guy from Seymour, Indiana, who got to write songs."

The *Uh-Huh* tour began with a curious premise, one that was antithetical to the most basic, bottom line instincts of show business—that the act get out there while the getting was good and play to as many people and make as much money as possible. Success, after all, is an elusive and transitory phenomenon: When you're hot, and you can sell concert tickets, you're hot; and when you're not, you can't even give them away. Even though John was now in a position to play to more people than ever before and book the largest venues, he bucked the easy money and opted for something else. "I didn't want people to think I was exploiting myself," he says. "On the *American Fool* tour I did 180 shows in big halls, and after 60 or 70, I hated it; I felt like a prostitute, working for the accountants. You can only take, take, take so much; I wanted to give something back. I wanted to play for the people who believed in me when nobody else did, who were there when I needed them, in intimate settings . . ."

The tour was a departure from anything he had done before. Before he even stepped onto the tour bus, the LP had already been out for five months, and John picked every date personally. Besides the usual big city stops, he directed himself through places like Florence, Alabama; Danville, Illinois; Davenport, Iowa; and West Lafayette, Indiana. "Sometimes he'd just pick a place on the map," recalls Ted Mellencamp, who road managed the tour.

"He'd say, *'That's* where I want to play. Find me a place to do it.' It was the first time he could ever say, 'Okay, now I'm gonna go out and play for *my* people . . .' "

His act was an astonishing spectacle: a white curtain opening to reveal the band on a simple, white, two-tiered stage, dressed in tuxedos, white shirts, string ties, white socks—like they were playing the senior prom. "It was John's idea to wear tuxedos, and the band bridled at first," says Mike Wanchic. "We felt like James Bond getting ready for the casino! Then we really got into it." The band would run forward, and out would prance John, an ear-to-ear grin on his face, who would fall into a wicked split, bounce up, grab the mike, and let it rip. No hype, no gimmicks, no overkill, no profanity—"He didn't swear once on the whole tour!" exclaims Ken Aronoff—nothing but scorching rock & roll.

The selection of songs opened with a thirty-minute medley of oldies before he even got to any of his own music, a lineup that included a rearranged, slowed down, heavy-grinding "Heartbreak Hotel"; Lee Dorsey's "Ya Ya"; the Animals' "Please Don't Let Me Be Misunderstood"; and an offbeat, captivating rendition of an obscure tune by the Left Banke, "Pretty Ballerina."

Gone forever was the exhibitionist with the chip on his shoulder, desperate to provoke the audience into responding to him. Instead, the audience saw a mature showman—gracious, uncharacteristically vulnerable, reaching deep into himself to bring every song to maximum life. His attitudes had changed so much that at first he hadn't wanted to do "I Need a Lover" because he now felt that the words were too coarse—too much of the old John. "Frankly, I felt embarrassed by a lot of the old material," he says. "You know, 'Hey, hit the highway,' all of that macho crap . . . But I knew people wanted me to do the song, so I let *them* sing the choruses themselves."

He introduced his own material by joking about the oldies he loved and saying, "Maybe twenty years from now people will say, 'Here's a song made famous by John Cougar Mellencamp,' " and then he would break into "Jack and Diane" to ear-splitting applause. Everywhere, the crowd became an integral part of the performance; on "Hand to Hold Onto," as on "I Need a Lover," he would let people in the audience actually sing the verses into his mike at the edge of the stage. He'd make fun of his recent rockabilly hairdo, with the swooping pompadour falling across his face: "There's a joke going around that the latest discovery in the rock world today is John Cougar's right eye." "Pink Houses" was solemnly dedicated to the unemployed, and when the roar after the song died down, he'd stand there and say, "Look, it's silly to

A fan's sketch of "Crumblin' Down".

With Joe Todd, on the porch of the Pink House.

run offstage, make the people applaud, and then run back onstage for an encore. I've been doing this for fifteen years, and it's just too pretentious. So I'll just go off for five minutes and go smoke a cigarette and then I'll be back for twenty more minutes!" Returning in a black T-shirt, he would close with "Golden Gates"; "Serious Business"; Richard Thompson's "Shoot Out the Lights," always referring to Thompson as "one of the best songwriters in the world"; "Hurts So Good"; and "Jackie O," an eccentric little cha-cha cowritten with John Prine for *Uh-Huh,* which turned on a wonderful bit of rhyming foolishness: "So you went to a party with Jacqueline Onassis/If you're so smart, why don't you wear glasses . . ."

What came across was the impression of an artist whose experience and growth were so inextricable from his audience that he could only put more and more of himself on the line as he became more successful. "There's a recklessness about him that turns raw edges into a very personal sort of passion," the *Chicago Sun-Times* perceived after John played the Arie Crown Theater. "He understands that success that rigidifies an artist's performance rather than liberating it is really failure—a failure of nerve. There's never been much question that he's got a lot of nerve . . ." His audiences responded in kind. In Kansas City, the show sold out in seven minutes. At the auditorium of Indiana University on February 16, the people were rocking out so intensely during "Authority Song" that the entire balcony started visibly bouncing up and down, causing hundreds of people in the orchestra to turn and stare in horror at the swaying structure. At Market Square Arena in Indianapolis, he was so moved by his reception that he could only stand there and say, "You don't know how this makes us feel." When somebody handed an Indiana state flag up to him, he unfurled the banner and brandished it around the stage like an Olympic standard before draping it proudly along the left of the stage, where it remained for the rest of the show. The crowd was screaming at the top of their lungs—as much for themselves as for the rock star who represented them up on the stage. "It was incredible—something this reviewer has never seen except in footage of concerts by the Beatles," wrote Steve Hall in the *Indianapolis News*.

Of course, such a welcome would be natural in John's home state; the real acid test came at New York's Radio City Music Hall, where John had scheduled a single performance on the night of April 10. The fact that the show sold out in two hours did little to ease his anxieties: New York was a city that he had yet to crack, a place that had never been kind to or even accepting of him, a town that he always associated with jaded concertgoers and cynical critics who were just waiting for him to fall flat on his face. "The night before

(Victoria Mellencamp)

in Poughkeepsie, everything had gone completely wrong,'' remembers Mike Wanchic. "Equipment blew up, everything just fell apart—a true-life nightmare. Fortunately, we got it all out of our system." "He gave us all a severe pep talk when we got into town," says Toby Myers. "He said, 'Look, if we never ever play good again in our lives, let's at least be good tonight.' "

Twenty minutes before the show, the band was upstairs at Radio City, dressed, watching James Brown's performance from the T.A.M.I. show on a video cassette. "That really psyched us up," relates Mike Wanchic. "We turned it off, walked right downstairs and straight onto the stage." By "Jack and Diane," the place was exploding. It was one of those truly special performances in the life of an artist when everything goes so well that the performer always walks a fine line between being completely in control and letting things get out of hand, when so much adrenaline pumps and courses through the band that the music seems to drop into overdrive and transcend itself. "My drumsticks were exploding in my hands," is the way Ken Aronoff remembers it. "Like they were playing themselves! I lost sixteen sticks that night." Prowling the perimeters of the hall, leaping gracefully from speaker to floor, John turned the most famous pop music venue in the world into his own private auditorium—the concert became his coming out party—and when he did "Play Guitar," parading down to the orchestra pit and snarling out the last verse—"All the women around the world want a phony rock star who plays guitar!"—it was clear that he had this audience now laughing with him, instead of at him. "For those of us who knew John when he couldn't even fill the Bottom Line," says Bill Cataldo, "it was like watching one of your children grow up." "I'd never seen that venue used so successfully for a rock and roll show before," Chris Connelly says. "He put on a hell of a show; he really filled that space and was clearly having a great time. People went in

(© Register and Tribune Syndicate, Inc)

"There's a joke going around that the latest discovery in the rock world today is John Cougar's right eye . . ."

expecting their minds to be changed about him and found them not only changed but overwhelmed."

"All the people who had once hated him came to the show," recalls Howard Bloom, "and after the show they were all grabbing me by the sleeve, going wild. The ironic thing is that John maintains that he hates performing, but when he gets on that stage he's like a transformed being. Backstage after the show, he was white as a sheet, trembling, with these huge eyes—'I'm never gonna do *that* again!' He always looks as though he never knows where he is after performing because he's just been through an experience where something much bigger than he is just picked him up and shook him around. It took him two hours to come back down to reality; we almost had to guide him around the room."

The tour was capped off with a performance at the Universal Amphitheater in Los Angeles, which was every bit as successful as the Radio City date. Word was getting out; the backstage area after the show was a veritable *Who's Who* of young Hollywood celebrities. After forty dates, everybody headed home, still savoring the experience, the din of the crowd still ringing sweetly in their ears. "It was the first time we ever didn't want a tour to end," says Larry Crane. "After that gig in LA, the feeling was, 'Is this *it?* I'm just getting warmed up!' "

Things would never be quite the same. The reviews and triumphant tour were a signal, a crucial signpost that John Mellencamp had reached only after a long journey; he had breached the final hold, reaching a place where "voice," "vision," and "responsibility" were the catchwords, where the issue was no longer simply feel but substance. The Kid Inside was now Spokesman for the Little Guy, one of Rock's First Citizens of Nowhere. It was all very flattering and more than a bit bewildering, even if the seeds had been there all along (just go back to *Chestnut Street Incident).* Like it or not (shades of Felicia Jeter!), he now had the mantle over his shoulders; no amount of self-deprecating charm or hayseed modesty could change the fact that people not only wanted to see him on a stage and listen to his records, but they wanted to know how he felt about the issues that affected their lives. He was not—and probably never would be—comfortable with fame, with being held up as a spokesman or example of anything ("I can't even keep my own personal life in order," he told a reporter, "how can I be an example to some kid on the street?"). The only question was how seriously he would take it all.

VI

SCARECROW

An Epilogue to a Story
Just Beginning

"Last night I figured out how many days I have
left in my life if I live to be eighty: something
like 17,155. Hey, surely I can waste a few of
them, right? But I feel guilty if I sit in
front of the TV for an hour—this is my problem
when I'm home. Of course, this never dawns on
me when I'm on the road—there's too much going
on at once, not enough time for myself. It all
boils down to finding the balances in life . . ."

"I've already got a place reserved in Seymour
where I'm gonna be buried. It's gonna be a
Plexiglas coffin, and I'm gonna be layin' in
it with a cigarette and a bottle of Big Red
and a TV on, and they'll come on every day and
change the chanels for me. At night it'll be
Channel 4 'cause they have movies 'til
dawn . . ."

Puttering around his kitchen in his bathrobe, John Mellencamp sticks the first
Marlboro of the day into his face, sits at the table with his morning coffee, and
asks, "Do you smell something funny? What does this place smell like to
you?"

The question is an obvious reference to the malfunctioning sewer system in
his home. The house is lovely, a renovated, enlarged two-story structure with
an indoor pool on acres of densely wooded land, complete with its own lake,
impeccably designed and decorated by Vicky Mellencamp and somebody who
John calls "some fancy dude from LA"—but the sewer system backed up,
and when you answer his question by saying, "Kind of like shit, John," he
gives you a dirty look, then sighs and takes a deep drag of the cigarette. "The

irony of it," he says, exhaling philosophically. "Here I am, finally with some dough, living in a nice house like this—and it smells like a cesspool!" He laughs raucously—that Mellencamp cackle, making his eyes go wide and bright. "Sort of puts the whole thing in perspective, don't it?"

"What do you want to eat?" asks his wife.

"Let me have one of those little Jewish deals," he says—meaning, of course, a bagel.

Teddi Jo Mellencamp, with white knee socks and black patent-leather shoes, an astonishingly beautiful and finicky three-year-old who John calls "little sister," fidgets while her father tries to get her to eat some breakfast. Paying his efforts little mind, she prefers playing with Griff, the huge German shepherd prowling the premises, waving his snout at her. John rolls his eyes helplessly.

"This is the longest I've been in one house, in one town, since I started making records," he explains. "I hardly know how to act! George Green tells me that the reason I am the way I am is because I have this fixation with death, and I have my goals set very high, so if I don't do something constructive every day, I go nuts—"

For close to two years, he's stayed home to work on his projects, watching from afar as the world turned toward other stars in the firmament of pop music: Prince, Bruce Springsteen, Cyndi Lauper, Madonna, and others. You could have easily spotted him speeding along the interstate in a perfectly restored 1956 Chevrolet Bel-Air, double-clutching and power-shifting and leaving rubber all over the road, with "Keep On Dancin' " by the Gentrys blaring from the tape deck, avoiding going back up to the little garage apartment at his home where he writes his songs—"I'm one of the great procrastinators of the Western World," he says. Other projects kept him busy, like the film project, "Ridin' the Cage," that he's developing at Warner's with Larry McMurtry, and director Jonathan Kaplan. He made the pleasant discovery that all sorts of interesting people wanted to work with him and, within one year, wrote songs for Barbra Streisand and the Blasters ("Can you think of two more drastically different types of artists?"). "It's been four months since we started *Scarecrow*," he relates. "The tracks were a breeze to lay down, but the mix has been agonizing—and now that the end is in sight, I've reached the point of being so inside the work that objectivity becomes more and more difficult."

Like every album in his career, *Scarecrow* serves a specific function: to bridge the gap between the mainstream commercial appeal of *American Fool* and the broadening, maturing songwriting sensibility of *Uh-Huh*. Instead of beginning the record with five or six songs and then writing and recording in a fury, he compiled over thirty songs. "I've been making records for nine years now," he observes, "and I'm just beginning to write for myself—to really hit my stride. A lot of things I've said have been misunderstood, and I realize now that's just because I didn't say them well enough. And it used to be, I always wanted to sound like whoever my favorite artist of the time was—I'd unconsciously pick up their mannerisms. I was really just a kid when I did most of my records . . . My whole self-image has really changed. Up until a couple of years ago, I had this romantic vision that I was this wild man, always trying to see myself as Brando in *The Wild One* or Dean in *Rebel Without a Cause*. I'm not that image—it's bullshit."

As a songwriter, John Mellencamp has become an inveterate gleaner from the real world, a sponge who is always susceptible to anything around him, always toying with phrases, ideas, words; if he hears or sees something, he's immediately humming it, talking about it, and the next time he sits down to write a song, it can easily filter into his writing. In addition, his wife has managed to organize him better. She bought him a typewriter, and he actually types out his lyrics now, collecting them in a black looseleaf book, which causes him to focus that much more intently on words and meaning. Of course, if you peer into the book and read his songs, you notice that *serious* is typed *sirious,* and quickly find other atrocities of spelling and syntax. The irony of this is not lost on one of his best buddies, Gary Boebinger, who still teaches high school English in Nashville, Indiana. "Here's a guy who flunked English his whole life, now he's a poet, right? It's like he's reliving all that time when he should have been studying in school, but was fucking off. Now he's really interested in politics, society, the economy—he watches news shows all the time, reads constantly . . ."

Scarecrow was recorded at John's newly constructed studio, a state-of-the-art facility located down Route 46, at a bend in the road called Belmont that offers all the basics: a gas station, a truckstop café, and a rinky-dink motel, which prompted John to dub the place "the Belmont Mall." As designed by Don Gehman and Gregg Edward, the studio means much more than the fact that he only has to travel fifteen minutes to work. "I want to make it available to new artists who might want to come out here and record," he says, "so they can hold their recording costs down. It might make it easier for an artist to be commercially viable at a record company at a time of soaring recording costs, when the companies are cutting back their rosters."

The music of *Scarecrow,* which positively drips with the feeling of the people and landscape of Indiana, has come powerfully together in the envi-

(Harvey Wang)

ronment that spawned the music. The singing, like the writing and musician-
ship, is passionate, phrased with more texture and subtle power than anything
that John has put on record. Many of the songs were written in a lower key,
which has allowed his voice more range; but an additional factor is that the
words themselves are more melodious, singable—more felt in the heart of the
singer. The sound is a perfect marriage of musical and technical simplicity: the
ringing guitars of Crane and Wanchic and Aronoff's thin, hard drumming,
accentuated by his high-pitched snare. The band, after years of developing in
a splendid musical isolation, has become like a living extension of the

songwriter, a pure instrument for the designs of his music. And with its hard floors and high rafters, there is little in the Belmont Mall to absorb sound—everything echos and bounds back at you. *Scarecrow* does not feature the processed sound found on most contemporary records, in which the music is pumped up in a hot mix to add bottom and to liven up the sound for the radio; instead, it conjures the spare sound of those R&B records cut by groups like Booker T. and the MGs at Stax in Memphis during the mid-1960s.

John Mellencamp has agonized over the mix of the album, but the agony was well worth it. Quite simply, he has made the best record of his life, with music that fulfills promises and represents the sum total of what he's learned and experienced. Each song provides a keyhole into the life and character of the songwriter and resonates with energy, thought, and depth of feeling. These are songs that cut and bleed and cry out and soothe and dance and get wild; that don't sound like anything else and not even like each other, for that matter.

After listening to the songs, you're tempted to tell him don't worry, John, you've really done it, broken through—just keep following your basic instincts with the mix and watch the whole thing keep rolling straight down the lane, like a bowling ball headed for a strike. You're also inclined to tell him how proud you are of him, because there are songs on this album that he's truly had to grow up to write, that show how far he's really come; but you don't say anything, because even if you did it wouldn't matter—it's not his way to believe such things. Just listen to the songs and hear him talking . . .

Blown-up bodies in the streets of Beirut, mounting war fever in Central America, chemical catastrophe in Bhopal—sitting with John Mellencamp in front of the nightly news and taking in the profusion of imagery is becoming an exercise in bitter cynicism. He admits to becoming a news junkie, but the reasons extend far beyond self-education or looking for song ideas. "I just want to know when I'm going to be blown up!" he says ruefully. "It's like Dylan said in a recent interview, 'The only peace man will know is when he is reloading.' I get depressed about everything that's happening. It's disheartening to be so young and idealistic and think you can change the world and find out by the ripe old age of twenty-one that you can't. Not only that, but the issues today are so immensely complicated—I can't make up my mind about how I feel about a lot of things, about which side to take—it keeps changing. That's why I'd just as soon stay away from politics . . ."

None of the songs of *Scarecrow* are explicitly political, yet they are, without a doubt, the most topical of his career. By the evidence of four songs on the album, he has embraced the terrain of "Pink Houses" with even more depth and passion, welcoming the challenge of saying what he feels about the world—but without preaching, by reacting in his own raw, instinctual way. He doesn't claim to have the answers. In a hard, ominous song called "You've Got to Stand for Something," he never says specifically what we should stand for, but through the litany of images, ranging from the Rolling Stones to Fidel Castro to a man walking on the moon to "I saw Miss America/ In a girlie magazine/I bet you saw that, too," the message becomes clear: You stand for your own truth, and how that truth relates to your experience of the world. Indeed, it becomes harder to know what's going on—only that something is going frighteningly awry.

> I know the American people
> Paid a high price for justice
> And I don't know why
> Nobody seems to know why

The chorus embodies not only his visceral reaction to what he sees going on around him, but a recognition of the need for him to take a stand in his own work—a clarion call to a new tough-mindedness, to a state of purpose and vigilance: "You've gotta stand for something/Or you're gonna fall for anything." The "anything" is totally openended—you can read your own fears and devils into it: false prophets and dangerous leaders and spurious rhetoric about war and peace, you name it. The only thing that Mellencamp is certain of is: "We've got to start respectin' this world/Or it's gonna turn around and bite off our face."

"The other day I was pumping gas into my car," John says, "and some guy comes up to me and says, 'Did you know that your property is one of the sites that they dumped chemicals on?' Did I about shit! You just can't get away from certain problems . . ."

Similarly, in "The Face of the Nation," a violently syncopated song with a tiptoe bassline by Toby Myers and an astringent acoustic break by Larry Crane, he uses the chorus to sketch a troubling vision.

> And the face of the nation
> Keeps changin' and changin'
> The face of the nation
> I don't recognize it no more

He feels helplessness in the face of what he sees: the broken dreams of lonely people being left behind by the changes he sings about; not the promises of a high-tech, high-opportunity society, but of more old people "Stumblin' their way through the dark," of little babies crying, of "people starvin' underneath the tree/And you wonder what happened to the golden rule." He sees sinister hands in the situation without identifying them, offering no concrete solutions but exhorting simple human perseverance.

> You know I'm gonna keep on tryin'
> To put things right
> If only for me and you
> Cause the devil is on our tail tonight

The music is breakaway rock, but harnessed to a deepening vision of a land and its people; the spirit of Bob Dylan echoes through the music, only the world that John Mellencamp is writing about is vastly different from the age that Dylan chronicled and heralded twenty years earlier in songs like "The Times They Are A-Changin'." Twenty years ago, people weren't losing their farms at the rate of one every five minutes. In "Rain on the Scarecrow," cowritten with George Green, the music reaches its most dramatic level with a subject that touches his very family, culminating in an anthem that will stand for a vanishing way of life.

> Scarecrow on a wooden cross. Blackbird in the barn
> Four hundred empty acres that used to be my farm
> I grew up like my daddy did. My grandpa cleared this land
> When I was five I walked the fence, while grandpa held my hand.

Stepping back, you see an artist who has chosen to take his strongest stands and chances at the moment when it would be easiest for him just to lay back and sit pretty.

In an era when people hunger for meaning in their music at the same time that they want to be diverted, *Scarecrow* connects John Mellencamp to a broad, growing audience. "His audience ranges widely," observes Kid Leo of WMMS, "about as big as you will find in rock—from sixteen to thirty-five. He definitely has his teen fans and girls who think he's sexy, but he's also one of the few artists where you're going to see thirty-year-olds at his concerts, who actually go out and buy his records."

John's relationship with his fans is enlivened by a special sense of shared

(Marc Hauser)

experience, precisely the feeling that allows people who don't personally know him to listen to his music or experience one of his performances and immediately feel an intimacy. People are forever coming up to him who feel that they "know" him, who want to tell him all about their lives, which both fascinates and baffles him. Truly, there aren't many performers who exert this particular appeal—most, in fact, keep an imperious distance. "To be on that stage and feel that affection is an awesome, humbling experience," he says. "It's like, wow, what did I do to deserve this? The feeling that comes over you is, 'What can I do to give this back to them?' So you're always reaching for that something extra, in your work, or on the stage . . ." Of course, it also means phone calls from some fan in Bloomington, waking him out of a dead sleep. John picks up the phone and hears a strange, laughing voice say, "Hey, man, how you doin'? You know something? I like you . . . You and me are the same people. Why don't you come on out to Jake's and we'll party!" To which John will say, "If you were like me, you'd be in *bed!* It's one o'clock in the morning!"

Scarecrow also reveals John Mellencamp to be, perhaps more than ever before, his own man. "He really does what he wants to do, instead of what's commercially right at the moment," emphasizes Chris Connelly. "What I like about him is that he's not a dogmatist. If he wants to do a screenplay, he'll do it; if he wants to cut a record in fifteen days, he'll do that too. What will always elude people who write about him is that he essentially operates on pure instinct. When he writes, he doesn't puzzle something out and worry if it's going to appeal to Adult Contemporary or whatever. It's his greatest strength."

"The thing about John that's amazing," says brother Ted Mellencamp, "is that nobody knows better than John what he should be doing at that moment. He hasn't even discovered how high he can fly yet; it's all ahead of him. I don't think he really wants to become this huge superstar, even if he could. There are so many things he could do—writing, producing records, acting, directing—and I think he'll do whatever he puts his mind to."

As bright as the future looks, don't get the idea that John is home free, that his life is all accolades and high-minded seriousness—or that he's completely at peace with himself. "He's found himself musically," recognizes Rus Shaw, "but emotionally, he's still searching. I've worked with a lot of people, and he's the most complex of them all." Explains guitarist Mike Wanchic, "John's always a live wire, and I never want to see him lose that edge. To me, it would be death if he turned into this totally mellow, stable guy."

Has John Mellencamp *changed?* George Green, who lives just down the

Portrait of John for *Scarecrow*.

road, mulls the question over. "He's got much more self-confidence and a much broader perspective of himself; he's much more able to control his emotions, but no, he hasn't changed that much." He pauses, chortles. "I take that back: He's much more polite than he ever was. He actually says *please* and *thank you* once in a while . . ."

"It gets harder and harder for him to relax and unwind," notes Mark Ripley. "It isn't as easy for him to have fun." Gary Boebinger, his other closest friend, makes the following observation: "He's happier than he was, but still not happy. Here's a guy who was once the epitome of a carefree spirit, who cared about nothing else but girls and music, who now realizes that the more success you have, the more success-related problems you have. And he's a hell of a hypochondriac. If he hears about a new disease, he's automatically got it!"

You can hear it in John's voice when he answers the phone: One day he's the essence of sunshine, the incarnation of human warmth; the next day Little Bastard rears his head. Flip the record over and you see radical mood swings, anxiety-ridden nights, a highly temperamental artist who is driven to tread the razor's edge of emotion, thriving on conflict, hellbent on doing things his own way, unpredictable, impulsive. Underneath everything else, however, is a vulnerability that comes from having a big heart—an unfailingly generous soul with a wonderfully demented sense of humor and an exuberant spirit.

John Mellencamp shrugs his shoulders at these observations. "People see me now and can't believe how calm I am compared to three years ago! It used to be that my struggle was all external, how I was going to do things in my career; now it's personal, private—inside of me. I recognize that I still have to learn how to find the balances in life. It's like a line in one of my new songs, 'Between a Laugh and a Tear': 'I know there's a balance, see it when I swing past . . .' "

What makes the John Mellencamp of today so vastly different from the John Cougar of five years ago is his ability, as a person and an artist, to manage his conflicts, drawing on them to imbue his work with humor, a poignant honesty, and a folksy wisdom. In "Rumbleseat," he writes about these very moods, contrasting the pits of depression with the times when he's "ridin' high/With my feet kicked up in the rumbleseat."

> Well I could have a nervous breakdown
> But I don't believe in shrinks
> I should be drunker than a monkey
> But I don't like to drink.

The theme of growing up reaches its emotional crescendo in "Minutes to Memories," a classic country/folk allegory cowritten with George Green, about an old man and a young man "on a Greyhound thirty miles beyond Jamestown." In a song that makes you feel like you're meandering down a lonely country road in a pick-up, the old man imparts what he's learned about life to the younger man; who in turn imparts the same message to his own son.

> Days turn to minutes
> And minutes to memories
> Life sweeps away the dreams
> That we have planned
> You are young and you are the future
> So suck it up and tough it out
> And be the best you can.

The lines contain the essence of a uniquely American spirit of forbearance, along with a complete system of traditionalist values embodied by the character of the old man, to be passed down through the generations.

> I worked my whole life in the steel mills of Gary
> And my father before me, I helped build this land
> Now I'm seventy-seven and with God as my witness
> I earned every dollar that passed through my hands
> My family and friends are the best things I've known
> Through the eye of the needle I'll carry them home

By the end of the song, the narrator—the younger man on the bus—comes to his own reckoning about the encounter, about the simple righteousness of the old man's life, who by now has long since passed away.

> The old man had a vision but it was hard for me to follow
> I do things my way and I pay a high price
> When I think back on the old man and the bus ride
> Now that I'm older I see he was right.

In "Lonely Ol' Night" we meet two estranged lovers, riven by unfulfilled needs and fears. The music is taut, brooding, a rending cry into the night. As their only means of salvation available, they still cling to each other. You can't help but see Jack and Diane fifteen years later, no longer young and innocent, now faced with the awesome predicament of finding and keeping love, left with the most profound dilemma of the human condition: "It's a lonely ol' night but ain't they all . . ."

With "Small Town," it becomes clear that *Scarecrow* is really a fully realized concept album about coming of age, a portrait of the life and times of the songwriter. The tune itself is introduced by an appropriate snippet of mood music called "Grandma's Theme," which features John on acoustic guitar accompanying his grandmother, Laura Mellencamp, as she sings an old folk tune called "The Baggage Coach." "I heard the song when I was a little girl," she says. "My Daddy used to sing it to me . . . It's about a guy riding a train with a little baby who's crying, and the passengers are telling her to be quiet. 'Where's the mother?' the passengers ask—it turns out she's in the baggage coach behind, in a coffin. It's the saddest song I ever heard in my life, and when John asked me to come into the studio, I was scared to death!''

> Well I was born in a small town
> And I live in a small town
> Probably die in a small town
> Oh those small communities

There is a sense of life and death, place and time, sadness and contentedness, youth and maturity—his life coming vibrantly alive in the music and words.

> All my friends are so small town
> My parents live in the same small town
> My job is so small town
> Provides little opportunity . . .

Now that he's famous, John Mellencamp could hang around with the elite of the music world, with movie stars and politicians—yet he prefers the company of Mark Ripley and Gary Boebinger. "He's always been that way," states Marilyn Mellencamp. "He isn't happy unless he's hanging around southern Indiana with his buddies. They entertain him and keep him down to earth. He's getting to be like Elvis was with his entourage." Just about his favorite thing in the world is sitting around, shooting the breeze with his friends, who are all intensely devoted to him. "No subject is ever taboo," says Gary Boebinger, "and he'll bring up everything—the more reason you have to hide something makes it that much better for him to bring it up. And you can always come to him with any of your problems—he's real good at giving advice and real bad at taking it . . ." The group has become something of an old-fashioned men's club. "We play snooker and poker," George Green says. "John cheats, everybody knows he cheats, and he knows everybody knows he cheats. It's gotten to the point where it isn't even worth it to stop the game and yell at him." His friends also provide a readily available pool of bodies for the impromptu football games that John holds in his parents' yard in Seymour, serious affairs known for bruised muscles and egos, which have become a Thanksgiving Day tradition. "A couple of years ago Ripley got so drunk on Thanksgiving that he just passed out on the ground," John says. "So we just used him for one of the touchdown markers. He rolled over once and that made it longer to go for a touchdown, but nobody really cared."

Still, his friends sometimes worry that John's situation will invariably cause him to feel that he has less and less in common with them. "It gets harder and harder for him to relate to a hundred dollars as being anything," says Gary

Visiting the Coliseum in Rome.

Boebinger. "What do we have in common with a rock star except the past? My wife Donna says that John thinks he's my father, always trying to take care of me. When I wrecked my motorcycle, he wanted to buy me a new one and I wouldn't let him. He said, 'You don't understand, Bo, I'd rather buy you a bike just so I can have somebody to ride with! That's worth much more to me than for you not to have any bike at all . . .' " Ripley echoes this concern. "We all have champagne tastes but we have to live on beer budgets—John, on the other hand, has a champagne budget. If he invites you someplace, you realize that you can't afford to pay for yourself and he pays and it gets to be kind of a drag. You get to thinking, 'All right, the only thing I know I can do for John is just be the best possible friend I can to him.' For all the stuff John does for me, what can I do for him?"

But John's friends are more than simply friends; they're also his conduit to the very America he's been writing about. He even gets ideas from their most casual talk. He'll say, "Goddamn, that's a great line!"—and take something from the most mundane conversation imaginable, turning it into a Top Forty song. And, most importantly, he can really let his hair down around his friends. Each year, all of them make a pilgrimage to Myrtle Beach, North Carolina; the guys leave the wives behind, and rent a Winnebago, hitching their motorcycles to the back, and get gloriously Neanderthal on the beach. His friends now jokingly refer to John as "the King" ("Elvis Mellencamp") and have no qualms about using "the kingly image" to reel in the girls on the beach like minnows, introducing themselves as famous rock musicians. "Oh, this is Bain, he played on the last Police album . . ."

"Oh *really*," the impressed girls will say. "What instrument do you play?"

"The McCullough," responds Bain, referring to the brand of chainsaw he uses to cut trees for a living back in Indiana.

> But I've seen it all in a small town
> Had myself a ball in a small town
> Married an LA doll and brought her to this small town
> Now she's small town just like me . . .

"When me and Vicky go to New York or LA now," says John, "it's like Ma and Pa Kettle go to the big city."

His marriage is a happy, successful one, though not without its volcanic moments. "They call me Jake LaMotta around here—the raging bull," John says jokingly of the arguments he has with his wife. "We have our biannual blowouts." John's friends refer to the couple as "Barbi and Ken," while John

John and Vick, with Russ Shaw on her right.

calls his wife "my partner," and for very good reason: She's always there for him, standing beside and supporting him, sharing everything. People who really know John Mellencamp can never say enough about Vicky and her patience and sensitivity, usually concluding with something like, "Poor Vick," or "I hope to God John doesn't blow it with her," etc. John is certainly no ogre, but with his mercurial moods and the ever-present pressures of the music business, he isn't the easiest person to live with. "I don't know how she puts up with him," Marilyn Mellencamp says. "When he gets in those moods of his, I'd tell him to jump if I was her!" But Vicky Mellencamp seems to have the perfect disposition for her husband's moods. She knows how to handle him. Several years ago, when John informed her that he was finally going to follow through and get a tattoo, she forbade him: "Oh, no you're not." "Oh, yes I am," John said. "If you do, I'll get my whole back tattooed," she told him, which stopped him cold—he knew that she'd do it.

Of course, the argument became moot since they decided to get tattooed *together,* John with a woodpecker and a broken heart that says *Forgive Us,* Vicky with a blue heron on her ankle and a tiny rendition of her husband on her shoulder. Indeed, Vicky is a down-to-earth woman with a rich sense of humor, who keeps Mr. Mellencamp on his toes. One night after an argument when John was in the shower, she went to investigate a rapping on the windows. It was three girls, all of them looking for "Johnny Cougar." "Oh, come on in," she said warmly. "He'll be *glad* to see you." When John emerged from the bathroom, a towel around his midsection, he found them sitting on his bed. "Honey, some of your fans would like to say helloo . . ."

His children are growing up so fast that it makes his head spin, providing a dimension to his life that leaves him endlessly amazed. "I really love being a father. It's important to me to have that in my life," he says, "because when you're an old man, you ain't got nothing except your kids. Your endeavors in the so-called business world are long gone, and all you've got is your family. Who's going to want to know about John Cougar Mellencamp when he's seventy? I'll be an old fucker with a bad prostate or something fun like that, listening to my old records and going, 'That's me.' *So what!* I hate to sound like Dorothy from the *Wizard of Oz,* but there's no place like home."

Michelle Mellencamp, soon to enter high school, has that Mellencamp strut, likes Bryan Adams, and lives sometimes with John and sometimes with Cil, who works for John as his "detail person" and lives in John's old house out at Lake Monroe. Both of her parents, considering their divorce, take pride in how well-adjusted Michelle is. "With Michelle it was never a big deal that I made records," John says. "She grew up thinking that everybody's dad was on the radio! I ask her about my records. I say, 'What do you think of my record, Chelle?' And she says, 'I like it, Dad.' And I know she fucking hates it. But what the hell, I never liked anything my old man liked . . ." Michelle has reached the age of adolescent revolution, a prospect that delights John's mother. "He's got his hands full with that one," Marilyn Mellencamp says. "He's going to be in the same position with her that I was with him—and I love every minute of it!" In fact, John recently admitted to stealing and secretly reading Michelle's diary—"I just wanted to know what she thought about things," he says innocently. One night not too long ago, after she returned from a night out with her friends, John asked her, "Well, where were you, out kissin' around with some guy?" When Michelle looked at John like he was out of his mind, he told her, "Ah come on, Chelle, you can tell me—I know what kids are like." Whereupon his daughter said, "Dad, I don't care what they did in the *olden days.*"

In the last couple of years, the family has moved closer into the orbit of his career, until they've become a sort of Mellencamp Family Rock & Roll Business: Brother Ted has road managed the tours, Cil runs the office in Bloomington, Tim Elsner keeps the books, cousin Tracy is a bodyguard, and even Aunt Toots has "Hurts So Good" tattooed on her thigh. Lately, Richard Mellencamp has come to look after his financial affairs.

His father's presence provides somebody that John can always count on, who always has his best interests in mind; the two of them have come a long way from the days when they were always at each other's throats. "I think that, a number of years ago, John started seeing me as a person, instead of his father," Richard says. "From that point on, we started to get closer and closer."

John and Marilyn, on the other hand, know how to push each other's buttons—and do so with good-natured relish. "Mom's still good lookin'," John says, "and stuck up as ever, always with an expression like somebody's holding a turd right underneath her nose. We both get bored easily so we decide to have a fight. If there's nothing to do, I'll say, 'Hell, why not go over and have a fight with Mom?' We can really get into it, and we don't pull punches. Hey, anything goes in a war! Our relationship is pretty comical . . ."

Seated in the small apartment above the garage where he goes to hide himself from the world and write songs, with his feet up on the table and his guitars perched around him like so many old friends, John Mellencamp laughs and takes a giant gulp of Big Red. "Now I realize how all the relationships in my life have really stretched me and helped me, fortified me," he says. "Just like, all the crazy things that happened to me were for a reason . . ." The words pour out of him in torrents, so fast when he gets going that he gets tripped up by his own sentences; the look that comes over him is not one of innocence or naïveté—it's the look of wonder, the look of a little kid who is ceaselessly amazed by the things in life that reveal us to ourselves, who has truly learned how to make the music say what's in his heart. It brings to mind a story that his family tells about him, about the night his grandfather passed away. John had always looked up to Speck Mellencamp, locating in the old man all of the qualities of resilient pride and individualism that he needed to fight his own battles over the course of his career. Perhaps these qualities are what allowed Grandpa to remain so robust in his last years, despite having lung cancer. He never lost that Mellencamp pugnacity: Only a few years before his death, he got into a fight at Uncle Joe's Rock-Sey Roller Rink and held his own. At his last chemotherapy treatment, while waiting for the doctor, he grabbed John's arm and whispered, "Come on, boy, let's go look at some of them young nurses!'' But the illness started to overcome Speck Mellencamp, and there was nothing that John could do about it, no matter how much the thought of losing the old man broke his heart. Sometimes on tour, John would realize that the time was getting nearer, and he would send a plane back to Seymour just to pick up Grandpa and bring him to the show, just to have him there; then it got so bad that Grandpa had to stop making the trip. On one of the few good days he had left before going into the hospital, John went to visit him at his house in Seymour, where the two of them sat out on the breezeway while Speck rocked back and forth and gazed out across the street at the cornfield. By that time, the old man was badly wasted by the disease, able to talk in only a hoarse whisper, but the two of them struck a kind of deal. ''Listen, Grandpa,'' John said. ''I can't take hospitals. I'm sorry, and I know you're gonna think I'm chickenshit, but when this cancer gets on top of you, I ain't going up there. I want to remember you the way you are. I just wanted you to know that.''

Speck looked at John for a moment and said, ''I understand, son. I wouldn't either if I were you.''

And so the two of them said good-bye.

On Christmas Day, the entire Mellencamp clan was gathered in Speck's hospital room, except for John. The scene is best recalled by John's grandmother, Laura Mellencamp. ''The door opened,'' she remembers, ''and in walked John, carrying his guitar. Everybody was surprised to see him because we knew that he didn't want to be there because of how much he loved Speck—he couldn't stand seeing him like that. John put his chair right up to my husband's bed and said, 'Now, Grandpa, I'm gonna sing you a song, okay?'—and my husband nodded. John sang him 'Silent Night.' He sang it so soft and beautiful, there wasn't a dry eye in the room—and then he left. That song was the best Christmas gift of my husband's life. He died that night . . .''

Like the songs go: *Oooh, yeah, life goes on, long after the thrill of living is gone. Walk on . . .*

The only promises I know to be true, are the promises made from the heart . . .

Days turn to minutes and minutes to memories. Life sweeps away the dreams that we have planned . . . You are young and you are the future . . . So suck it up and tough it out . . . And be the best you can .

John and Speck.

(Marc Hauser)